MAYER SMITH

The Witch's Heart

Copyright © 2024 by Mayer Smith

All rights reserved. No part of this publication may be reproduced, stored or transmitted in any form or by any means, electronic, mechanical, photocopying, recording, scanning, or otherwise without written permission from the publisher. It is illegal to copy this book, post it to a website, or distribute it by any other means without permission.

This novel is entirely a work of fiction. The names, characters and incidents portrayed in it are the work of the author's imagination. Any resemblance to actual persons, living or dead, events or localities is entirely coincidental.

Mayer Smith asserts the moral right to be identified as the author of this work.

Mayer Smith has no responsibility for the persistence or accuracy of URLs for external or third-party Internet Websites referred to in this publication and does not guarantee that any content on such Websites is, or will remain, accurate or appropriate.

Designations used by companies to distinguish their products are often claimed as trademarks. All brand names and product names used in this book and on its cover are trade names, service marks, trademarks and registered trademarks of their respective owners. The publishers and the book are not associated with any product or vendor mentioned in this book. None of the companies referenced within the book have endorsed the book.

First edition

This book was professionally typeset on Reedsy.
Find out more at reedsy.com

# Contents

| | | |
|---|---|---|
| 1 | The Mysterious Visitor | 1 |
| 2 | The Hidden Letter | 7 |
| 3 | The Shadows in the Forest | 13 |
| 4 | Into the Depths | 19 |
| 5 | The Echo of the Heart | 25 |
| 6 | The Heart's Vein | 31 |
| 7 | The Binding Ritual | 37 |
| 8 | The Hollow Echo | 43 |
| 9 | The Veil Between | 49 |
| 10 | The Other Side | 55 |
| 11 | The Hollow Heart | 61 |
| 12 | The Breaking Point | 67 |
| 13 | The Unraveling | 73 |
| 14 | The Choice | 79 |
| 15 | The Price of Power | 86 |
| 16 | The Reckoning | 92 |
| 17 | The Broken Bond | 98 |
| 18 | A Thief in the Night | 104 |
| 19 | The Price of Power | 111 |
| 20 | The Return of the Dark | 117 |
| 21 | The Echoes of Fate | 123 |
| 22 | The Depths of the Heart | 128 |
| 23 | The Silent Promise | 134 |
| 24 | The Unraveling | 139 |

| 25 | Beneath the Surface | 145 |
| 26 | The Price of Freedom | 151 |
| 27 | Fractured Souls | 157 |
| 28 | The Hunt Begins | 163 |
| 29 | A Heart's Betrayal | 169 |
| 30 | The Final Choice | 175 |

# 1

# The Mysterious Visitor

The fog hung thick over the village, wrapping around the cobblestone streets like a suffocating blanket. It was the kind of mist that crept into the bones, leaving everything shrouded in mystery. Lily had always been sensitive to the strange energies of the land, but tonight, it was different. She could feel the weight of something ancient pressing down on her, its presence lurking in the silence. The wind whispered in a language she didn't understand, urging her forward, but she couldn't shake the feeling that she was being watched.

She stepped lightly, her boots tapping against the wet stones as she made her way down the winding path that led from her cottage to the village center. The distant glow of lanterns flickered like dying stars, their light barely piercing through the dense mist. There were few people about this late, the village settling into an eerie calm, but Lily's senses were on high alert. She felt the pulse of the earth beneath her feet, the subtle rhythm of magic that hummed in the air.

As she rounded the corner near the old well, a figure appeared in the shadows. The man stood tall, almost unnaturally so, his silhouette outlined against the dim glow of the lanterns. His presence was striking—he seemed to belong to another time, another world. The way the fog curled around him, almost as if it was drawn to him, sent a chill down her spine.

Lily hesitated, her instincts screaming at her to turn back, but something in the man's gaze held her in place. His eyes were an unsettling shade of silver, glowing faintly in the night, and they seemed to pierce right through her. His hair, dark as the midnight sky, framed a face that was both handsome and otherworldly, with sharp features that hinted at a life lived far beyond the ordinary. His clothing was odd too—dark, almost too formal for the simplicity of the village, and adorned with symbols she couldn't recognize.

"Are you lost?" Lily asked, her voice steady despite the unease gnawing at her. Her words felt strange in the thick silence, like they were swallowed up by the fog before they could even reach him.

The man didn't answer right away. Instead, he studied her as if weighing her every feature, every detail. His lips barely moved when he spoke, his voice a low, melodic whisper that seemed to come from everywhere and nowhere at once.

"I'm not lost," he replied, his tone sending a shiver through her. "But I believe you are."

Lily's heart skipped a beat. She instinctively took a step back, her senses brimming with confusion and curiosity. Was this man... a stranger? Or had she seen him before? The feeling of familiarity gnawed at her mind, as if he belonged to her past—a past she couldn't remember clearly, no matter how hard she tried.

"Who are you?" she asked, though part of her feared the answer. She felt like she should know, as if his name was on the tip of her tongue.

The man smiled, a subtle, knowing grin that made the fog around them swirl with an unnatural energy.

"I am someone who has been looking for you," he said, his gaze never leaving hers. The words were laced with something she couldn't define—an urgency, a purpose that felt both ominous and strangely comforting.

Lily felt a chill crawl up her spine. "Looking for me?" Her voice faltered despite herself. "Why?"

His smile deepened, but his eyes darkened in response. "Because there are things about you, about your family, that you have yet to understand. Things that must be discovered, before it is too late."

Lily's pulse quickened. There was a strange weight to his words, an invisible force pressing against her chest, threatening to suffocate her. Her mind raced, trying to connect the dots, but nothing seemed to make sense.

"You don't know what you're talking about," she said, her voice growing firmer as she fought the growing sense of dread. "I'm just a—"

"Just a girl from the village?" he interrupted smoothly, his tone never changing. "You are much more than that, Lily. And there are forces at work that you cannot yet see. You will soon understand."

Lily felt her breath catch. Her name—he knew her name. How? She hadn't given it to him. How could he know her?

The fog thickened, swirling around them, and Lily's heart began to race faster. She stepped back, her instincts telling her to get away, but the man's presence rooted her to the spot. She didn't understand why, but she felt an undeniable pull toward him, a connection that felt ancient, as though their fates had been intertwined long before this moment.

"What do you want from me?" Lily asked, trying to steady her voice, but failing.

The man stepped closer, his movements fluid and almost predatory. "What I want, Lily, is for you to come with me. There is much to explain, and not much time left. The witch's heart is calling to you. It's calling to all of us."

The words hit her like a physical blow. The witch's heart? Her grandmother had spoken of it in whispers, in riddles, but she'd always dismissed it as a family legend, nothing more.

"The witch's heart," she repeated, her voice barely audible. The fog seemed to hold its breath.

"Yes," the man said softly, his gaze darkening with something far older than the fog around them. "The witch's heart. And you, Lily, are the key to it. You will find it—or it will find you."

Lily's stomach churned, and she stumbled back, tripping over the uneven ground. "I don't know what you're talking about," she said desperately, but the man's expression remained unreadable.

He moved forward quickly, his hand reaching out for hers, his fingers brushing against her skin. For a brief, fleeting moment, she thought she felt something—something pulsing beneath her skin, as if his touch had ignited something deep within her.

"I know you're scared," the man said, his voice now a soft murmur that seemed to echo around them. "But you can't run from your destiny. The heart is coming for you. You don't have a choice."

Before Lily could respond, he stepped back, disappearing into the fog as quickly as he had appeared. The mist swallowed him whole, leaving only the echoes of his words behind.

Lily stood frozen, her breath coming in shallow gasps, her mind a whirlwind of confusion and fear. The village around her was silent once more, but the air felt heavier, charged with something unknown.

The witch's heart. The words echoed in her mind like a distant bell, calling to her, pulling at something deep within. She didn't know what it all meant, but she knew one thing for certain: her life had just changed forever. And whatever was coming next, she wasn't ready for it.

But she had no choice.

# 2

# The Hidden Letter

Lily couldn't sleep that night. The man's words echoed in her mind like a curse, refusing to be silenced. "The witch's heart is calling to you." She tossed and turned in her bed, the room heavy with the oppressive stillness of the village. The fog had lingered, clinging to the rooftops and creeping through the cracks of her windows like a silent predator.

She had tried to push the encounter from her thoughts, tried to convince herself that the stranger was nothing more than a figment of her imagination, some phantom conjured by the eeriness of the fog. But deep down, she knew better. There was something undeniable about the way he had looked at her, as though he had been waiting for her all along.

The witch's heart. It wasn't just some idle legend her grandmother had muttered about in her more eccentric moments. It was real—too real. And now, it seemed to be pulling her into its web.

In an attempt to distract herself, Lily got out of bed and crossed the room, reaching for the old wooden chest that sat against the far wall. Her grandmother's belongings had been passed down to her after her death, a collection of dusty, forgotten treasures from a life she had barely known. Lily had always been drawn to the chest, though she never quite understood why. It was an inheritance she had never asked for—an inheritance she wasn't sure she wanted.

As she opened it, the scent of aged paper and lavender filled the air, comforting yet unsettling. The dim light from the single candle flickered across the contents, illuminating faded letters, photographs, and trinkets that seemed to whisper forgotten memories. But it was one letter, buried deep beneath a stack of old maps, that caught her eye.

It was a thick parchment, its edges frayed, as though it had been handled countless times over the years. The seal on the envelope was broken, and the ink on the paper had begun to fade, but the words were still legible.

Lily's fingers trembled as she unfolded the letter. The handwriting was elegant, looping and precise, a stark contrast to the hurried scrawl of most of her grandmother's notes. The words seemed to pulse with an energy all their own, a language that was both familiar and foreign.

She squinted at the first few lines, struggling to make sense of the strange symbols written at the top. It was a language she had never seen before, one that felt ancient, forgotten, like a secret that had been passed down through the generations.

The rest of the letter, however, was in a language she could understand.

"To the last of the bloodline," it began, sending a chill through her chest. "The heart calls to you, as it did to your ancestors before you. You are not safe. The darkness that follows the heart is relentless. It will stop at nothing to claim what is rightfully its own."

Lily's breath hitched. She glanced at the symbols at the top of the letter again, feeling an unsettling connection to them, as if they were meant for her to decipher.

"The witch's heart is not a mere artifact," the letter continued. "It is the source of an ancient power, a power that binds us all. If you are reading this, then the time has come. You must find the heart before it finds you. It lies hidden, locked away in a place only the bloodline can uncover."

Lily's hand shook as she read the next few lines. The letter spoke of a curse, one that had haunted her family for generations. A curse tied to the heart of a witch who had been both revered and feared. And now, it seemed, the heart was calling to her, drawing her into a destiny she had never asked for.

The letter went on, describing a ritual—a ritual that could either break the curse or seal her fate forever. There was no middle ground. The heart had to be destroyed, or it would destroy everything.

She read on, but the words began to blur together, the weight of what she was reading too much to bear. She pressed her hand to her forehead, trying to steady her breathing, but it felt like the walls of the room were closing in on her.

Then, she saw something that made her freeze.

At the bottom of the letter, written in a hurried scrawl, were three words that stood out against the delicate handwriting.

"Trust no one."

The letter slipped from her fingers, falling to the floor with a soft rustle. Her pulse quickened as she stood motionless, the room now heavy with an unfamiliar tension. Her grandmother had always spoken in riddles, but this was different. This wasn't just cryptic nonsense. This was a warning.

Lily could feel the weight of those three words pressing down on her. Trust no one. The thought echoed in her mind, as if the letter itself had planted the seeds of doubt in her heart. She had always trusted the people in her life—the villagers, her friends, her family—but now, she wasn't so sure.

A noise from outside the window broke her reverie, a faint scratching sound against the glass. Lily's head snapped toward the sound, her heart racing in her chest. The fog outside had thickened, and the darkness seemed to stretch out further, creeping toward her. Was it the wind, or was someone—or something—watching her?

Her pulse quickened as she stepped toward the window, but

before she could pull back the curtain, she heard a faint knock at the door.

Knock. Knock. Knock.

The sound was deliberate, slow, and rhythmic. It sent a shiver down her spine.

Lily's breath caught in her throat. She hadn't been expecting anyone. Not tonight.

Cautiously, she moved toward the door, her every step deliberate and quiet, as if trying to avoid being heard. Her hand hovered over the doorknob, but she hesitated. Was it him? The man from the fog? Or was it someone else, someone who had come to find her?

With one final glance at the letter on the floor, she opened the door.

To her shock, no one stood there. The dark hallway outside was empty, eerily still. But there, lying on the doorstep, was a small parcel—wrapped in dark brown paper and tied with twine.

Lily's heart pounded in her chest. She bent down slowly, her hands trembling as she picked it up. The weight of the package seemed wrong—too heavy, too solid. She unwrapped it carefully, her mind racing, her breath shallow. Inside, there was a small wooden box, intricately carved with symbols she recognized from the letter.

It was the same symbol.

The witch's heart.

She couldn't breathe. This wasn't a coincidence. This was too much, too soon.

With shaking hands, she opened the box. Inside was a pendant—a heart-shaped stone, dark as night, with veins of silver running through it like cracks in the earth. It pulsed with a faint, rhythmic light.

Lily felt the air around her grow colder, the room heavy with an unseen presence.

And in that moment, she knew with certainty—her life had just become far more dangerous than she could have ever imagined.

# 3

## The Shadows in the Forest

The air felt different the next morning. The fog that had clung to the village like a suffocating shroud the night before had lifted, but something remained. An unnatural stillness, a sense of waiting, hung in the air. Lily's hands shook as she tucked the small wooden box into the hidden drawer beneath her bed, where it would be safe—for now. She couldn't shake the image of the heart-shaped stone pulsing with its eerie glow. What did it mean? What had she just uncovered?

The events of the previous night seemed unreal, like fragments of a dream she couldn't fully remember. But the pendant was real, and so was the letter. And the man—the stranger in the mist—his words burned in her mind like a warning she couldn't escape. "The heart is coming for you." She shivered just thinking about it.

Lily knew one thing for certain: she couldn't stay in the village any longer. The danger was too close, too immediate. But where could she go? The answer came to her in a flash—the forest. Her grandmother had always spoken of it, telling stories of how the woods held ancient secrets, hidden places where time seemed to stand still, untouched by the modern world. But there was more to it than that. The forest had been a sanctuary, a place where she could escape, where the pull of the unknown didn't feel so suffocating.

Lily grabbed her coat, her boots, and without a second thought, she set out toward the woods.

The path to the forest wound through the village, past the cobblestone streets that were eerily quiet in the morning light. No one was out, not even the birds sang. It was as though the entire world had fallen silent, waiting for something to happen. She could feel the eyes of the village on her, even if she couldn't see them. The shadows seemed to follow her, pressing in on her from every side.

When Lily reached the edge of the woods, the silence deepened. The trees, tall and twisted, loomed over her, their branches like dark, gnarled hands reaching toward the sky. The wind whispered through the leaves, but there was no warmth to it. It felt cold, like it carried secrets with it—secrets that only the forest knew.

Lily stepped into the forest, her boots sinking into the damp earth. The air was thick with the scent of moss and decay. The path was narrow and winding, the trees growing closer together, blocking out the sun. She moved deeper, feeling the pull of the woods around her, the sense that she was being drawn into something she didn't fully understand.

A strange noise broke the silence—a low, rasping sound that seemed to come from all around her. Her heart skipped a beat, and she froze, listening intently. The sound was like breathing, deep and uneven, but it didn't belong to anything she could see.

Lily's breath came in shallow gasps as she scanned her surroundings. Her senses were heightened, her body alert, every instinct telling her that something was wrong. The air felt thicker now, heavier with an invisible pressure. She couldn't explain it, but it was as though the very forest itself was watching her.

Then, without warning, the noise stopped.

Lily took a step forward, cautiously, but her feet felt heavier with each movement, as though the ground was pulling her in, urging her to stay. A faint rustle came from behind her, and she whipped around, heart racing. But again, there was nothing. The forest was still, impossibly still.

"Get a hold of yourself," she muttered under her breath. But the words didn't help. The silence was deafening.

As she ventured further into the heart of the forest, the trees began to change. The trunks twisted, bending at odd angles, their bark black and slick with dampness. The ground beneath her feet was uneven, patches of thorny vines and brambles making the walk even more treacherous. Lily's fingers brushed against the cold, damp bark of a nearby tree, her touch sending a shiver through her spine. It was as though the forest had become a living thing, something sentient that was aware of her every move.

She stumbled over a root and caught herself just before falling. A low growl echoed from somewhere nearby, but it wasn't an animal's growl. It was something deeper, more guttural. Something that felt wrong.

Lily's pulse quickened, and she instinctively reached for the pendant hidden beneath her coat. Her fingers brushed the smooth surface, and for a moment, she thought she felt it pulse in response, as if it were calling to something in the forest. She hesitated, unsure if the feeling was real or just her mind playing tricks on her. But she didn't have time to dwell on it.

She quickened her pace, pushing forward through the dense underbrush, until she came to a clearing. The sunlight barely filtered through the thick canopy above, casting everything in an eerie, muted glow. At the center of the clearing stood an ancient stone structure, half buried in the earth. It looked like a temple, or perhaps an altar—old, forgotten, and covered in moss. But what drew Lily's attention was the carving on the stone, faint but visible in the dim light.

It was the same symbol as the one on the pendant. The heart-shaped design, etched deep into the surface of the stone, surrounded by intricate runes. The carving seemed to pulse with a faint, unnatural light, just like the pendant.

Lily stepped forward, drawn to it as if by an invisible force. Her fingers traced the edges of the carving, and as they did, the earth beneath her feet trembled. A low rumble vibrated through the ground, and the air seemed to thicken, charged with a strange energy.

Suddenly, a figure emerged from the trees.

Lily's heart leaped into her throat as she spun around. The figure was tall, draped in dark, flowing robes, their face obscured by the hood. For a moment, she thought it was the man from the village—the stranger—but something about him felt different. His presence was more ominous, more menacing.

The figure moved forward, slow and deliberate, and Lily instinctively took a step back. The pendant around her neck began to glow brighter, and the man—or whatever he was—stopped.

"You shouldn't be here," the figure said, his voice smooth, cold, like the sound of a stone scraping against stone.

Lily's breath caught in her throat. She couldn't explain why, but she knew this man—this creature—was connected to everything. The pendant, the forest, the witch's heart. It was all connected, and now, she was standing at the center of it.

"Who are you?" she demanded, her voice shaking but determined.

The figure didn't answer immediately. Instead, he raised his hand, and the ground beneath Lily's feet shifted. The earth cracked open, revealing dark, swirling tendrils of energy that seemed to reach for her, pulling at her, like the forest itself was alive and hungry.

"You are too late," the figure said, his voice growing darker. "The heart will claim you, just as it has claimed so many before you. It's already too late to stop what has been set in motion."

Lily backed away, her heart hammering in her chest, the pendant around her neck pulsing with an intensity that made her feel like it was alive. She wasn't sure what to do—what to say. She didn't understand any of this, but one thing was clear: the forest, the figure, the heart—they were all part of the same thing. And that thing was coming for her.

Her breath came in shallow gasps, her thoughts a whirlwind of confusion and fear. But before she could react, the ground beneath her feet gave way.

And everything went black.

# 4

# Into the Depths

Lily's eyes snapped open, but the world around her was shrouded in a darkness so complete, it felt like the air itself was smothering her. Her chest tightened with panic as she tried to move, only to find herself lying on something cold and uneven. Her limbs felt heavy, as though the ground beneath her was trying to pull her deeper into the earth.

She gasped for breath, struggling to push herself up, but the air was thick and oppressive. Every movement felt like wading through molasses. As she sat up, her fingers brushed against a stone surface. The ground beneath her felt smooth, but old—ancient even. The stone was damp and covered in a strange, slick coating that made it hard to keep her balance.

She looked around, but the darkness was so consuming, she couldn't see more than a few inches in front of her. Her pulse raced in her ears as she reached for the pendant around her neck, its familiar weight reassuring against her skin. But it was warmer than it had been earlier, almost too warm, as though it were alive—throbbing in rhythm with her own heart.

Something was wrong. She could feel it.

The air shifted suddenly, a gust of wind that stirred the stagnant darkness, and with it, the smell of damp earth and something else. Something foul. A sickly-sweet odor, like rotting flowers, filled her nostrils, making her stomach churn. It was then that she realized, despite the suffocating stillness around her, she was not alone.

There was movement. Soft and careful, like someone—or something—was walking, their footsteps muffled by the stone floor. Lily's breath caught in her throat, and she instinctively reached for the small dagger her grandmother had left her. It was tucked into the waist of her coat, a precaution for the nights when the forest seemed more dangerous than usual. Her fingers closed around the cold hilt, and for the first time since she'd entered the woods, she felt a tiny flicker of control.

A low growl echoed through the darkness. It was primal, deep, vibrating in her chest like the rumble of distant thunder. Lily's body tensed, and her eyes darted to the shadows that shifted around her, almost too quickly for her to track. The growl came again, closer this time, but it was not the growl of an animal. No, this sound had a human edge to it—too low, too controlled.

Her heart pounded in her chest, the sensation growing louder in her ears. She could barely breathe, the fear suffocating her. Her eyes scanned the dark, searching for the source of the sound, but all she could see was the black void that surrounded her.

The pendant around her neck pulsed again, a warm throb, like a heartbeat. And then it grew hotter—too hot, searing her skin.

Lily yanked the pendant from beneath her coat, staring at the stone as it glowed fiercely, almost painfully bright. The dark tendrils that had emerged from the earth seemed to recoil from the light, shrinking back into the shadows like a wound being cauterized. But even as the pendant pushed back the darkness, the growls grew louder, more insistent, until they were almost deafening.

Something was coming.

She jumped to her feet, every nerve in her body screaming for her to run, but there was nowhere to go. The walls around her pressed in, smooth and unyielding. There were no doors, no windows—just the oppressive, endless stone. She turned in place, trying to steady herself, trying to find any way out, but the weight of the air was growing unbearable.

And then, the figure emerged.

A shadow shifted from the corner of her vision, moving so fluidly, it was almost like it was part of the darkness itself. Slowly, a form began to materialize—a tall, dark shape with glowing eyes that pierced the night. It was humanoid in shape, but something about it was wrong. Its limbs were too long, its movements too smooth, too deliberate. It stepped forward, its form becoming clearer with each passing second, but it never fully left the shadows.

Lily's heart raced. The creature was dressed in tattered robes, much like the figure she had encountered in the forest. Its face was obscured by a dark hood, but she could see the faint outline of a face beneath it—pale, gaunt, with sharp features that seemed to shimmer in and out of existence, as though it were not fully corporeal.

A voice, cold and hollow, echoed through the chamber.

"You shouldn't have come here, child."

Lily's breath hitched, and her body froze. She didn't know if it was the creature's voice or the way it resonated in her very bones, but it felt like a command, a force that compelled her to remain still. The figure's glowing eyes flickered as it moved closer, the air thickening with each step.

"What are you?" Lily managed to whisper, though her voice trembled with fear. She held the dagger tightly in her hand, though she knew it would do little against whatever this thing was.

"I am the guardian," it replied, its voice reverberating like the sound of distant thunder. "The keeper of the heart. And now, you are the chosen one."

Lily's throat tightened, and her hands shook. She had no idea what this creature was talking about. The heart. The witch's heart. Her heart. The words felt like a weight on her chest, suffocating her.

"No..." she whispered, shaking her head. "I don't understand."

The figure stepped forward, and the air around Lily seemed to shift, charged with energy. It moved closer still, until it was standing right before her, its cold eyes boring into hers. The pendant on her neck pulsed again, warmer this time, and the creature hissed.

"You should have never found it, child," the creature said. "But now that you have, it's too late. You are tied to it. Bound by blood. The heart will call you, no matter where you go. It is a curse. You cannot escape it."

Lily's mind raced. She couldn't breathe. The forest. The pendant. The curse. It was all coming together, but it made no sense. She didn't want this. She didn't want to be bound to the heart, to whatever evil this creature represented.

The figure's lips curled into a twisted smile, its teeth sharp and pointed, gleaming in the darkness. "The heart is coming for you. And there is no hiding from it. There is no escape."

Lily took a step back, her pulse thundering in her ears. She glanced around wildly, searching for anything that could help her. But all she saw was the endless stretch of stone, the darkness pressing in from all sides.

The figure reached out, its hand long and bony, like a skeleton's. It moved too fast, and Lily barely had time to react before the cold fingers wrapped around her wrist, pulling her toward the center of the room.

Her heart raced, and panic surged through her veins. The dagger. She tried to raise it, but the figure's grip was unbreakable. The warmth from the pendant seemed to be fading, leaving her feeling cold and weak. She had to get away. She had to—

A sudden crack echoed through the darkness.

The ground shook beneath her feet, and the stone beneath them began to split open, long fissures appearing in the walls. The figure's grip faltered, and Lily took her chance.

She yanked her arm free, twisting violently out of the creature's grasp, and bolted toward the nearest gap in the stone. The floor was buckling beneath her, the earth itself reacting to the presence of the heart.

The figure's voice echoed through the chamber, cold and mocking. "Run, if you must. But remember, the heart calls to you. It will always call."

Lily didn't look back. She couldn't.

The darkness was closing in again, the air thick and suffocating, but she ran faster than she ever had before. And somewhere deep within the bowels of the earth, the heart pulsed, calling her name.

# 5

# The Echo of the Heart

Lily's breath was ragged, her legs burning from the effort of running, but she couldn't stop. She couldn't afford to. Every instinct told her to keep moving, to escape whatever nightmare had ensnared her. The darkness felt alive, pressing in on her from every side, but still she ran, her feet pounding against the stone, desperate to outrun the suffocating air, the cold tendrils of fear that wrapped around her like chains.

She didn't know how much time had passed. The darkness swallowed her, leaving no trace of where she'd been or where she was going. The stones beneath her feet shifted as if the very ground was moving, pulling her deeper into the labyrinth of shadows. But still, she ran, not knowing where she was headed, only knowing that if she stopped, she might never move again.

The air seemed to grow colder, the silence pressing down on her with an unbearable weight. She could hear her own heartbeat, the frantic pulse pounding in her ears, but there was no other sound. No footsteps following her. No whispering wind. Just the echo of her own movements, the hollow click of her boots on stone.

Then, a sound.

A faint whisper, like the flutter of wings, distant and soft at first, but it grew louder, closer. The air around her seemed to shift, the temperature dropping further. A chill crept up her spine, and her skin prickled with a coldness that made her want to scream. But she swallowed the fear, forcing herself to keep moving.

The whisper turned into a voice, low and insistent, reverberating through the stone walls. It was familiar—too familiar. She recognized it now. It was the voice from the forest, the voice of the figure who had warned her.

"The heart calls, Lily."

She stopped dead in her tracks, the breath knocked out of her. How did it know her name? How could it—

The air shifted again, this time with purpose. The stone underfoot cracked, a deep, rumbling sound that made her stumble back. She spun around, eyes wide, heart thundering in her chest.

There, in the darkness, something moved.

A figure emerged from the shadows, tall and imposing, draped in a cloak of shadow, their features hidden beneath a hood. The form was a silhouette at first, but as it moved closer, Lily could see the outline of a face—a face that seemed to shimmer, as though it were formed from the very darkness around them. The eyes, those glowing eyes, were all she could focus on.

"You can't escape it," the figure whispered, the words filling her mind like a dark promise. "It has chosen you. The heart is already within you."

Lily took a step back, her breath coming in short, panicked gasps. "What do you want from me?" Her voice cracked as she spoke, her body trembling. She gripped the pendant tightly in her hand, but it felt strangely warm, almost hot to the touch, as though it had a life of its own.

The figure's lips parted, revealing sharp, gleaming teeth that reflected the dim light, and a low, almost musical laugh escaped them.

"What do I want?" The voice was low, laced with a dark amusement. "I want you to understand that you are no longer in control. The heart has awoken, and it will lead you to the depths."

Lily's pulse quickened. "The depths?" Her mind spun as she tried to make sense of the words. "What does that mean?"

The figure took a step forward, the stone beneath its feet creaking as though it were alive. "The heart calls, Lily. It calls to you, and you are bound to it. You cannot outrun what is within you now. You cannot escape."

She shook her head, trying to block out the terror that rose in her chest. She had to get away. She had to leave. The walls were closing in. She could feel the presence of the creature pressing against her, suffocating her, and she was certain that if she didn't leave this place now, it would be too late. She reached for the dagger hidden in her coat pocket, fingers trembling, but as she gripped the hilt, a strange force seemed to push back against her. The blade felt like it weighed a thousand pounds, its power drained by the oppressive darkness around her.

"You can't fight it," the figure said, its voice now a cold, mocking whisper. "You're not strong enough. The heart is already inside you."

Lily's chest tightened, and the world around her seemed to blur, the edges of her vision fading as the figure's words echoed in her mind. The heart was inside her? No. She didn't want this. She couldn't have this curse, couldn't be tied to this dark thing. But even as she thought it, the pendant burned against her skin, hot and heavy. It was as if it were alive, pulsing in time with her heartbeat, calling to her.

The figure moved closer, its form seeming to stretch unnaturally, the shadows around it writhing like serpents. Lily wanted to scream, to run, but her body wouldn't obey. She was rooted to the spot, her legs too heavy, too sluggish, as if they were being weighed down by the very earth beneath her.

"You cannot run from the heart," the figure repeated, its voice now like the scraping of nails on stone. "The heart that beats within you, the heart that you awakened. It will claim you, Lily.

And when it does, there will be no escape."

Lily's breath caught in her throat, her vision beginning to darken around the edges. The darkness itself seemed to grow deeper, thicker, until it was all she could see. She couldn't think, couldn't move—her body felt as though it was being swallowed by the very shadows she feared. The pendant around her neck throbbed with a force that was almost painful, and her pulse raced to match it.

And then, without warning, the darkness exploded outward, sending a wave of raw power through her body. The figure stumbled back, its eyes widening in shock as the energy that had been coiling around Lily suddenly surged with unstoppable force.

Lily gasped, her entire body jolting forward. The pendant flared brightly, a blinding light that sliced through the shadows. The air around her vibrated, charged with a force that shook the very walls. And for the first time since she had entered the forest, she felt a surge of something else—something deep within her, something fierce and untamed.

She wasn't powerless.

The figure recoiled, the shadows around it seething, and Lily felt her body move on its own, as though some force greater than her was guiding her. Her hand shot out, her fingers brushing against the air, and the darkness recoiled again, this time with a hiss of pain. The figure staggered back, its hood falling away to reveal its face—pale and gaunt, with skin that seemed to stretch too tightly over the bones. Its eyes glowed with an unnatural light, and its mouth twisted into a grimace of anger.

"You are stronger than I thought," it growled, its voice filled with malice. "But it won't be enough."

The darkness surged once more, and the figure lunged, its hands reaching for her. But Lily was faster. She raised her hand, and in that moment, she felt the pulse of the pendant deep within her chest. A roar of power erupted from her, raw and uncontained, and the shadows shrank back, recoiling in fear.

For a brief, heart-stopping moment, Lily felt like she was in control.

But then the ground trembled again, and the air grew thick with an ancient power, one that she could feel pulling at her very soul. The heart was calling her—louder now, clearer now—and she knew, without a doubt, that whatever this force was, it was far from finished.

The figure's eyes blazed with fury, its mouth twisted in a snarl. "The heart will claim you, whether you are ready or not."

Before Lily could react, the shadows surged forward, and she was swallowed whole. The darkness consumed her, pulling her into its depths.

And the heart's echo followed her, louder and louder still.

# 6

## The Heart's Vein

Lily's breath came in shallow, panicked gasps as the darkness tightened around her, pressing in from all sides. She could feel the coldness seep into her very bones, the chilling air freezing her lungs as though the shadows themselves were inhaling her life force. Her feet no longer touched solid ground, and she had the distinct feeling of falling, though her eyes saw only blackness.

She fought against the sensation of being lost, trying desperately to calm her breathing, her fingers clawing at the air around her, searching for something—anything—solid to grasp. There was nothing. No wall. No floor. No ceiling. Just the abyss, a seemingly endless chasm that seemed to stretch infinitely in every direction. The darkness was so deep, so complete, that it felt like she was trapped in the very center of the universe, alone.

Her mind was spiraling. She had no sense of time. No sense of place. It felt like she was being drawn into the core of something ancient, something primal. The heart—the heart that had been calling to her, the one she had tried to run from. It was here. Somewhere, deep inside her.

The pendant around her neck burned, its heat intense, almost scalding, but it wasn't the warmth of the sun or even fire. It was something else. A relentless, pulsing heat that felt as though it was being drawn from the very marrow of her bones. She clenched her teeth, her fingers grasping at the necklace in an attempt to pull it away, but it was as if it had fused with her skin.

The voice came again. It wasn't the figure from before, but it was no less terrifying. This voice was soft, almost tender, but its words sent a jolt of dread through her chest.

"Lily..."

It was her name. But it wasn't her grandmother's voice. It wasn't the voice of someone she trusted. It was something darker. Something older.

"Lily, come closer."

The command was not spoken aloud. It was inside her head, inside her very soul, like a whisper buried in the marrow of her bones. She could feel it curling around her thoughts, sinking into her veins like a poison that she could not shake.

"No," Lily whispered hoarsely, her lips trembling as she struggled to maintain control. "I won't listen."

But the voice persisted, gentle, coaxing, insistent.

"You were always meant for this. The heart is yours to claim. You can feel it, can't you?"

A wave of nausea hit her, and she staggered, her knees threatening to buckle beneath her. The heat from the pendant surged again, almost as though it were trying to force its way into her chest, to take root where her heart should be. The pulsating rhythm it had once shared with her own heartbeat was now overwhelming, deafening. It was everywhere, filling the void.

She couldn't breathe.

Suddenly, her vision flashed. A shimmer of light, like a crack in the blackness, appeared before her. At first, it was so faint that she wasn't sure if it was real. But it grew—slowly, at first, a faint golden glow that expanded with each passing moment. Then, it burst open like a door breaking free from its hinges, spilling out warmth, brightness, and the unbearable pressure of something ancient, something alive.

Lily stumbled forward instinctively, her body moving before her mind could catch up. She knew she shouldn't—knew that every instinct should scream at her to stay away, but the pull was undeniable. It was a call that bypassed reason, bypassed her will, and latched onto something deeper, something buried beneath her fear.

The crack in the darkness widened, revealing a cavernous space, its ceiling stretching far above her in jagged, stone formations.

The walls were slick with some kind of black substance that shimmered in the light, as if the very stone itself were alive. The air was thick, heavy with an oppressive energy that seemed to throb in time with her heart—no, with the heart inside her. The heat from her pendant was unbearable now, and Lily could feel it, an intense pressure deep inside her chest, as though her own heart were growing, expanding, transforming into something else entirely.

In the center of the cavern, standing in a pool of flickering light, was a stone pedestal. It was ancient, covered in strange runes that seemed to shift and move beneath her gaze. The air around it hummed, vibrating with a power that made the hairs on the back of her neck stand on end.

And there, resting upon the pedestal, was the heart.

It was not like any heart she had ever imagined. It was not a beating, living thing, but rather an object—smooth and pulsing with a faint golden glow. It seemed to breathe, its rhythm mimicking that of her own heart, and yet it felt far older, far more alive, than anything she had ever encountered.

Lily's breath caught in her throat. She could feel its presence, like an electric charge in the air. The pull was stronger now, almost unbearable. Her feet moved of their own accord, stepping forward toward the pedestal, her hands trembling as they reached out to touch it. But the moment her fingers brushed the surface of the stone, a sharp, searing pain shot through her arm, and she recoiled, stumbling backward.

The voice came again, now louder, more insistent, as though the heart itself was speaking through it.

"Take it, Lily. Claim it."

The ground trembled beneath her feet as a low, rumbling growl echoed through the cavern, rising from deep within the earth. The shadows on the walls seemed to stretch and writhe, twisting into monstrous shapes. Figures began to emerge from the darkness, their eyes glowing with the same golden light as the heart. They were humanoid but twisted—tall, gaunt figures with skin that seemed to pulse like the heart itself.

Lily took a step back, her breath quickening, heart hammering in her chest. She had to get away. She had to—

But the heart pulsed again, and with it, the earth itself seemed to respond. The shadows closed in, trapping her in the center of the cavern. She could hear the figures moving closer, the soft scrape of their feet against the stone. Her pulse quickened, the heat from the pendant unbearable now. It was like a weight pressing against her chest, suffocating her, pulling her down into the depths of the earth.

She tried to move, but the world seemed to be closing in on her. Her vision blurred as the figures surrounded her, their golden eyes locked on her. And then the voice came again, louder, insistent.

"Take the heart, Lily. It is your birthright. You belong to it now."

Her hand trembled, moving once more toward the pedestal. She didn't want to. She couldn't. But she had no choice. The heart was inside her now. It was calling to her, claiming her, and there was no escape.

Her fingers brushed the edge of the stone once more, and this time, the pain didn't come. Instead, the moment her skin made contact, the world around her exploded in light.

The heart pulsed. The cavern trembled. And Lily was no longer sure if she was controlling her own body or if it was the heart that had taken over.

And somewhere, deep within the darkness, the echoes of the heart grew louder.

# 7

# The Binding Ritual

Lily's fingers trembled against the heart, the golden warmth seeping into her palm like molten fire. The cavern around her quaked, sending reverberations through her entire body. The heart beneath her hand pulsed in time with the rhythm of her breath, as if it was alive—and it was alive, she realized, with a sentience older than the earth itself. The moment her skin made contact with its surface, a sharp, jagged pain coursed through her arm, a feeling not unlike being struck by lightning.

She gasped and jerked her hand back, but the heart refused to let go. It was as if invisible chains had wrapped around her wrist, pulling her toward the pedestal. Her vision blurred and swam in front of her eyes. A voice, soft and haunting, whispered within her mind.

"You are mine now."

Her breath hitched, and the walls of the cavern seemed to shift, drawing closer with every passing second. The figures that had surrounded her now stood at the edge of her sight, their golden eyes glimmering in the dim light. There was no escape. They were closing in, waiting for something. Waiting for her.

The air grew heavier. The shadows deepened, curling like living tendrils at her feet. The heart beneath her palm throbbed harder now, and Lily could feel the weight of it, the ancient power emanating from it, seeping into her very soul. A cold dread gnawed at her insides, a feeling she had never known before. It wasn't just fear—this was something deeper. It was as though the very marrow of her bones knew the gravity of the situation, knew that nothing would be the same once she touched it.

What had she done?

"Take it," the voice said again, but this time it was different. It wasn't gentle, nor coaxing. This time, it was demanding, insistent. "It is yours to wield. Accept it."

Lily felt the urge to rip her hand away, to run, to leave this place behind and forget everything that had led her here. But even as she thought it, the pain of resisting surged through her chest, and her body moved of its own accord. Her fingers clenched tightly around the heart, and in that instant, everything around her seemed to stop. The shadows grew still, as if time itself had paused.

A sharp intake of breath filled the silence. She wasn't alone. Something else was with her.

The figures that had surrounded her began to chant in a language she could not understand. Their voices rose in eerie unison, melding together like a sinister melody, an incantation as old as the earth. It wasn't words—at least not in the sense that she could comprehend—but the sound itself sent tendrils of fear creeping up her spine.

The cavern seemed to shift once more. Beneath her feet, the stone began to glow, faint markings emerging like veins pulsing with the same golden light as the heart. The symbols spread outward, carving themselves into the stone with a sound like thunder rolling in the distance. Lily's heart hammered in her chest, each beat louder than the last, drowning out the chanting around her.

And then it happened.

The world around her cracked open.

A blinding light shot up from the heart, enveloping her entirely. It was like nothing she had ever experienced. The light burned, but it didn't hurt. It filled her completely, consumed her mind, her body, until there was nothing left but the pulse of the heart and the rising chant. And then came the sensation—like her body was tearing apart from the inside out, as though she were being pulled into two separate places at once.

No!

She screamed, but there was no sound. The light around her flickered, and suddenly, the pain surged again, deeper now, darker. A sharp, wrenching agony tore through her chest, and she thought she might suffocate on it. It was as though something was pulling at her very soul, dragging it toward the pedestal, pulling her into the heart's beating, relentless rhythm.

She tried to pull away. She tried to scream, but no sound came. Her legs buckled beneath her as the cavern's walls seemed to close in tighter, pressing against her from all sides.

The chanting grew louder, as if the very earth itself was singing the words now. There was no escape. The heart had begun its binding ritual, and Lily was at the center of it.

With an earth-shaking roar, a crack split the air, and the heart surged violently in her hands. A wave of unbearable force hit her, knocking her to the ground. She could hear the figures moving now, their forms shifting in the shadows, but she could not look up. She could only focus on the unbearable pressure in her chest—the pounding in her head as if her skull would burst.

And then the world went still.

The light vanished.

The cavern became eerily silent, the chanting subsiding as if the ritual had been completed. Lily lay on the ground, gasping, her body trembling, but the pain had lessened. She could feel the presence of the heart inside her, like a weight in her chest, a constant reminder of its power, its unyielding grip.

Her hand was still clenched tightly around the heart. But it no longer pulsed in her grasp. Now, it seemed to merge with her own heartbeat, its rhythm becoming indistinguishable from her own. She could feel it, deep within her chest, as if it were alive inside her.

It was in her. It was part of her now.

Lily forced herself to sit up, every part of her body screaming in protest. Her chest ached with the aftershocks of the ritual. She didn't know how long she had been lying there, but when she finally opened her eyes, the figures were gone. The cavern was empty, the oppressive shadows lifting, leaving behind nothing but the faint glow of the markings on the stone walls.

Her eyes fell to her hand, still holding the heart. It was no longer just an object. It was hers. But the moment she acknowledged it, a shudder passed through her, a cold wave of realization that the heart was not a gift—it was a curse.

Something in the distance shifted, and Lily's head jerked toward the sound. The shadows moved again, flickering like living creatures. There was something more, something still lingering in the air, a presence that had not yet revealed itself.

And that presence was growing stronger. It was watching her.

Lily scrambled to her feet, her legs shaky beneath her, but the pull of the heart inside her chest kept her anchored. She couldn't run. She couldn't hide. She had taken it, had bound herself to it, and now there was no escaping the consequences.

The voice that had haunted her for so long returned, this time cold and distant.

"Now the true path begins."

A chill ran through her, and Lily turned her back on the pedestal. She didn't know what that meant—the true path—but she was certain of one thing: the ritual was only the beginning. The heart had claimed her, and now, whatever forces had been unleashed would stop at nothing to ensure that she fulfilled her role in its dark design.

Lily didn't know where to go, or what would happen next. But one thing was clear: she was no longer just a part of this world. She was a part of something much, much darker. And it was only a matter of time before the true cost of the heart's power would make itself known.

The binding ritual was complete. Now, the reckoning would begin.

# 8

## The Hollow Echo

Lily couldn't remember how she had left the cavern. One moment, she was standing before the pedestal, the pulsing heart binding itself to her in ways she couldn't comprehend, and the next, she was outside—blinking against the harsh brightness of the moonlight filtering through the trees. The dense forest surrounding her felt oddly familiar, yet foreign, as if it had changed since her last visit, as if something deep within the earth had shifted.

Her legs were unsteady, and her breath came in quick, shallow bursts, as though she had been running for miles. She looked around, trying to ground herself, but the silence was unbearable. The usual hum of the night—the chirping of insects, the rustling of leaves—was gone. There was only an eerie stillness, a thick, suffocating quiet that felt unnatural, almost deliberate.

She stumbled forward, her feet dragging through the underbrush as she moved deeper into the forest, her heart pounding relentlessly. The pendant still burned against her skin, its warmth intensifying with each step she took, a constant reminder of the heart's power inside her. Her chest tightened as the weight of her actions sank in. She had claimed it. She had bound herself to something that was not human, something ancient and powerful, and now she was trapped within its grasp.

A soft, rustling sound came from the bushes behind her. She froze, her body tensing, the hairs on her neck standing on end. It was faint at first, like the whisper of wind moving through the trees—but then it came again, louder, unmistakable. Someone—or something—was following her.

She turned, her heart thumping in her ears, but saw nothing. Just the trees, their long, skeletal branches reaching out like fingers in the moonlight. Still, the feeling of being watched did not dissipate. It was as if the forest itself had become aware of her presence, aware of what she had done.

Lily pressed on, her legs trembling with each step, the woods seeming to stretch on endlessly before her. She didn't know where she was going—only that she had to keep moving. There was no safe place to rest, not now. She could still hear the soft, distant chanting in her mind, the words that had flooded her consciousness during the ritual. It wasn't in any language she recognized, but they had felt like promises—or threats.

Then, as she rounded a bend in the trail, she saw it.

A figure stood at the edge of the clearing, motionless. The moonlight glinted off the pale skin of its face, making it seem almost ethereal, like a ghost. The figure was tall, cloaked in flowing black robes that billowed out like shadows. Its face was obscured by a hood, but Lily could feel its eyes on her, cold and unblinking.

For a moment, Lily thought she might be dreaming—perhaps this was some manifestation of the heart, a trick her mind had conjured to torment her. But no. The air was too thick with tension, too real, for it to be a dream.

The figure tilted its head ever so slightly, as if examining her, before it spoke in a voice so smooth, so chilling, that it sent a wave of ice through her veins.

"You have begun the ritual, but you have not completed it."

Lily's stomach dropped. She opened her mouth to speak, but no words came. The figure's presence was overwhelming, as though it wasn't just in front of her—it was all around her, filling her senses, drowning her in its cold certainty.

"What... what do you want?" she finally managed, her voice hoarse.

The figure did not answer immediately. Instead, it stepped forward, moving with an eerie grace, its feet barely touching the ground. Lily instinctively took a step back, but the figure's presence seemed to close the distance between them effortlessly, as though it were in control of the very air.

"You have taken the heart, girl," the figure continued, its voice laced with both menace and a strange sort of reverence. "But it is not enough to claim it. You must open the door."

"The door?" Lily repeated, confusion and fear mingling in her chest. "What door? What are you talking about?"

The figure did not answer. Instead, it reached up with one long, pale finger and pointed toward the trees. Lily followed the gesture, her heart racing, but all she could see were the dark shapes of the trees and the faint glimmer of moonlight through the branches. There was nothing out of the ordinary. Nothing but the haunting silence.

"The door," the figure repeated, its voice now softer, more insistent. "The heart has already called you. You must open the door, or the forest will never let you leave."

Lily's stomach twisted in a knot. The words seemed to rattle around in her mind, echoing like hollow thunder. The forest. The door. What was it trying to tell her?

She took another step back, the figure's gaze never leaving her. The closer it got, the more she could feel an unnatural cold pressing against her, as though the very air around the figure had frozen.

"You don't understand," it said, a trace of something dark in its voice now, almost pitying. "You've begun the journey, but there are others who will come for you—others who will stop at nothing to take what you've claimed. The heart belongs to them, and they will do whatever it takes to return it to its rightful place."

Lily felt a chill run down her spine. Her mind reeled with the weight of the figure's words. The heart belongs to them. Others will come.

"You don't have much time," the figure continued, its voice growing more distant, as if it were drifting away. "The door is the only way to protect yourself from the forces that are already stirring. You cannot hide from them, not here, not in this place. The heart has chosen you, and the blood it has spilled will stain your hands forever."

With that, the figure slowly began to fade into the shadows, its form dissolving like smoke on the wind, leaving Lily standing alone in the clearing, her chest heaving with panic.

But the sense of being watched only grew stronger.

The trees began to move—slowly, imperceptibly, as if they were aware of her every move. Their branches stretched, reaching toward her, as though they were closing in. She could hear the sound of footsteps now—light, quick, and too many to count. The air around her thickened again, growing oppressive, heavy with the weight of something terrible.

And then she heard it: a whisper, faint but unmistakable, riding on the breeze.

"Open the door, Lily."

Her heart pounded in her chest as the whisper grew louder, closer. The world around her seemed to blur, the edges of reality fraying as though the very fabric of time had begun to unravel. She wasn't sure if she was still standing in the clearing or if the world had changed entirely.

She didn't know what the door was, or where to find it, but she knew one thing for certain now: she had no choice. She had already set everything in motion, and there was no turning back.

Something was coming for her, and it would not stop until it had what it wanted.

Lily turned and ran, the thundering footsteps growing louder behind her. She didn't know where she was going—only that she had to find the door before it was too late.

# 9

# The Veil Between

Lily's legs burned with every step, her breath ragged as she sprinted through the dense underbrush. The trees, which had once been familiar to her, now seemed to close in around her, their gnarled limbs twisting like dark fingers reaching down from the sky. The whispering voices had begun again, soft at first, but now rising in a cacophony, swirling around her like a storm.

"Open the door, Lily."

The words were inescapable. Each time the voices spoke, they grew louder, more insistent, until they felt as if they were inside her head, clawing at her thoughts, gnawing away at her sanity. But no matter how fast she ran, no matter how desperately she pushed herself, the forest seemed to stretch on forever.

Her heart hammered against her chest as she stumbled over roots and rocks, the forest floor slippery with dew. She couldn't stop. Not now. Not when she felt the pressure closing in around her, when the trees seemed to lean in with an eerie sentience, watching, waiting. The shadowy figures from the cavern seemed to follow her, their presence thickening in the air, just beyond her reach. Every rustle in the leaves, every snap of a twig beneath her foot made her pulse spike with terror.

"Where is it?" she gasped, choking on the dry air. "Where is the door?"

There was no answer. The forest didn't reply—only the rising whispering grew louder, more frantic.

She needed to find it. The door. Whatever it was, she had to open it. But how? The figure in the clearing had spoken of a door, but no matter how much she tried to recall the details, the memory felt like shifting sand in her mind. She didn't know where it was, or how to unlock it. But she knew one thing: there was no escaping without it. The heart had tied her to something ancient, something beyond human understanding, and if she didn't open the door, if she didn't finish whatever the ritual had begun, she feared she would lose herself to it forever.

The trees thinned ahead, and for the first time since she had fled the clearing, the whispers quieted. The silence was deafening, oppressive. She slowed, her breaths coming in short gasps, eyes darting around as she tried to make sense of her surroundings. The moonlight was still sharp in the sky, casting long, skeletal shadows across the ground, but everything felt wrong. The forest had become a labyrinth, each turn unfamiliar, each shadow darker than the last.

And then she saw it.

A shadow, flickering at the edge of her vision, just at the base of a towering oak. It wasn't a person—not quite—but something else. A shape, a movement that didn't belong in this world. Her blood ran cold.

The air grew heavier, thick with an unnatural energy, and the ground beneath her feet seemed to tremble with the weight of something ancient and powerful. It was there, standing just beyond the oak, a dark figure wrapped in a cloak of shadow. Lily's chest tightened as she took a step forward, her body frozen in place. She knew she had to move, had to get closer, but her legs refused to obey. The figure felt like a wall, something solid and unyielding in the darkness.

Then it spoke.

"You cannot outrun what you have become, Lily."

Her stomach flipped at the voice—soft, melodic, yet terrifying in its cold finality. It wasn't just a voice. It was something that echoed within her very being, reverberating in the deepest parts of her soul.

"You're not real," Lily whispered, her voice trembling. She squeezed her eyes shut for a moment, trying to clear the fog in her mind. It's just an illusion, she told herself. Just a trick of the forest.

But when she opened her eyes again, the figure was still there, its presence unwavering.

The figure took a slow, deliberate step toward her, the shadows swirling around it like a living cloak. Lily's heart rate spiked. She couldn't stay here. She couldn't face whatever this was.

With a sharp intake of breath, she forced herself to turn and run again, her feet pounding against the earth. But as soon as she moved, the whispers returned—louder, closer. They were everywhere now, filling her ears, clawing at her mind. She could feel the very air itself pressing against her, thick and suffocating. The forest was no longer just a backdrop. It had become a prison.

The trees shifted as she ran, bending and twisting unnaturally, the shadows deepening as if the darkness itself were alive. The ground beneath her feet began to crack and split, black fissures appearing in the earth, threatening to swallow her whole. She leapt over the cracks, her heart in her throat, the forest seeming to close in around her.

Suddenly, the ground beneath her feet gave way. Lily screamed as she plunged into the abyss, the world spinning around her. The wind whipped at her face, and she reached out, grabbing at anything she could find. Her hands scraped against stone, cold and jagged. She tried to pull herself up, but the edges were too slippery, the ground too unstable.

Her body collided with something solid, and the world stopped spinning. She gasped for air, her chest tight, and opened her eyes to find herself lying on cold stone, the darkness pressing in around her. The forest had disappeared.

She was no longer in the woods. She was in a cavern—a dark, hollow space, the walls slick with moisture, the air thick with the smell of earth and decay. There was no sound, not even the whispering voices. It was as if the world had fallen silent, and only the echo of her breath remained.

Her fingers brushed against the stone floor, and she froze. The sensation under her touch was different—smooth, unnaturally smooth, as if the stone had been polished by something more than just time.

Her eyes darted around, and in the dim light, she saw it: a door.

It was enormous, carved into the stone with intricate runes and symbols that twisted and writhed like living things. The air around it shimmered, like a heatwave, but it was colder than any winter night. There was no handle, no lock, just an empty frame, the doorway itself seeming to pulse with an energy that made the hairs on the back of her neck stand on end.

The door. The one the figure had spoken of. The one she had to open.

Lily moved toward it, her legs weak, but her resolve hardening. The pendant around her neck warmed, as though the heart inside her was reacting to the door, responding to its call. She reached out, her hand trembling, and as her fingers brushed the air just before the threshold, a sharp jolt of pain shot through her chest, the heart inside her racing in time with her pulse.

And then, like a rush of wind, a voice echoed from within the stone:

"Step through, Lily."

She swallowed hard. The door wasn't just a passage—it was a choice. A choice she had to make, or risk losing herself to the shadows forever.

Lily took a deep breath, her heart thundering in her chest, and stepped forward, her foot crossing the threshold.

The world shifted.

The door slammed shut behind her.

# 10

# The Other Side

Lily's breath came in ragged gasps as the world around her twisted, warped, and folded like paper. The air buzzed with static, as though reality itself was flickering, hesitating between dimensions. Her body was pulled forward, as if dragged by some invisible force, her feet barely touching the ground, her skin prickling with a sensation she could not describe.

The door behind her vanished into darkness, leaving no trace, no indication that it had ever existed. In its place, there was nothing but endless shadow and a faint, sickly glow emanating from deep within the space before her. The air was thick with an unnatural humidity, the scent of earth and decay overwhelming her senses.

Her hand, still clutching the pendant, burned against her skin. The heart inside her chest throbbed in rhythm with the pulse of the strange place she now inhabited, as if it were alive, feeding off the very energy around her.

Her heart skipped a beat. Where am I? The thought clattered in her mind like a storm. This was no longer the cavern she had emerged from, nor the forest where she had run. This was something different—something old, ancient, and deeply wrong.

The ground beneath her feet shifted. The stone beneath her shoes cracked with an audible snap, and she froze, her gaze snapping downward. The cracks spread outward, reaching in every direction like veins, pulsing with a dark, red light, as though the earth itself was alive and bleeding.

And then the whispers returned.

They were no longer distant. They were close—too close. The voices surrounded her, rising in volume with every passing second, like a choir of shadows, a thousand different tones, each one rasping and gasping, but never speaking clearly. They filled her ears, her mind, her very soul.

"You shouldn't have come."

The voice was unmistakable—cold, low, and filled with an ancient bitterness. Lily spun, her eyes searching the endless shadow around her, but she could see nothing. There were no shapes, no figures. Just the oppressive darkness.

"You are not meant to be here, Lily." The voice echoed again, louder this time, like a physical presence, shaking the very air around her.

A scream bubbled in her throat, but she choked it down, forcing herself to stand still. Her eyes darted around, desperate for any sign of life, any clue as to where she had ended up. The glowing light was dim, faint, but it cast long, grotesque shadows that seemed to slither and writhe along the walls. The shadows... no, they weren't shadows at all. As Lily watched in horror, they began to take shape—slowly, deliberately.

Figures began to emerge from the darkness—tall, skeletal shapes with eyes that burned like molten gold. They moved toward her, their limbs unnaturally elongated, their faces devoid of expression, their mouths open wide in a silent scream. They were not human. They were something else, something older, something that had been waiting for her.

The heart within her chest began to thrum, its rhythm picking up pace. The figures continued to advance, and she felt the pressure in her chest grow unbearable, as though the heart was calling to them, drawing them closer with every beat.

"You are the key."

The words came again, not spoken, but felt, deep within her mind. The voice was everywhere now, surrounding her. Her chest tightened, and she gasped for air as she stumbled backward, her legs shaking with the effort. She didn't understand. She couldn't understand. The heart—the ritual—it had to be the key, but to what? What was this place? And why was she here?

One of the figures, its face still a blur of shifting shadows, reached toward her with a long, skeletal hand. Lily recoiled, but her body wouldn't obey. She couldn't move. She was rooted to the spot, frozen by a force she couldn't comprehend. The figure's fingers brushed against her skin, and a jolt of electricity shot through her, filling her with an overwhelming sense of dread.

The figure leaned in, its breath cold against her ear. "It is time."

A wave of nausea swept over her. She could feel the darkness pressing in from every side, closing around her like a tomb. The whispers were louder now, too many voices, too many words, each one more incomprehensible than the last. She felt as though her mind was splintering, breaking apart under the weight of their demands.

"You must open it."

The voice was no longer distant. It was inside her mind, clawing its way into her thoughts, twisting her reality. She couldn't breathe. She couldn't think. She could only feel the heart inside her, pulsing relentlessly, demanding, pulling, and pushing all at once.

Suddenly, the ground trembled. The shadows, the figures, the whispers—they all seemed to stop, as if they were waiting for something. The air around her thickened, crackling with power.

Then, with a violent snap, the world around her shifted again.

The darkness fractured, breaking apart like shattered glass, revealing a new scene. The walls of the cavern dissolved, replaced by a vast, endless expanse of empty space. In the distance, there was something—an object, an anomaly, something that called to her with an indescribable pull.

It was a door.

But this was no ordinary door. It was enormous—twice the height of a person, its frame twisted and bent in unnatural shapes, the edges glowing with an eerie, sickly light. Runes etched into the surface seemed to writhe and change before her eyes, shifting as though alive.

It was the door. The door she had to open.

Her chest ached with the knowledge. The heart inside her had been leading her here all along, to this moment. She could feel it now—the pull, the energy coursing through her veins, urging her forward. But there was something else, something darker in the air.

The figures had not followed her. But something else was watching. Something far worse.

She hesitated for just a moment, then took a tentative step forward, her foot scraping against the cold, smooth surface of the stone. The moment she did, the ground beneath her trembled again, this time with more intensity. The whispers returned, louder now, all around her.

"You shouldn't open it."

The words were sharp, angry, filled with a venomous warning that sent a chill down her spine. But she couldn't stop. She couldn't. The heart burned hotter inside her chest, and as she reached for the door, a sharp pain exploded through her skull. She fell to her knees, gasping for breath, her vision darkening at the edges.

But then—just as the world seemed ready to swallow her whole—she touched the door.

The moment her fingers brushed against the cold surface, the door flung open, and the world around her shattered.

Darkness poured through the threshold, a torrent of shadows, a flood of ancient power rushing in like a wave. Lily's screams were swallowed whole as she was pulled into the abyss.

# 11

# The Hollow Heart

Lily's vision blurred, the edges of her consciousness fraying like old fabric. She could no longer feel her body, no longer hear the world around her. The only sensation that remained was a cold, gnawing emptiness that pressed down on her chest, making it difficult to breathe. It was as though the very air was thick with despair, suffocating her with every breath.

A sudden rush of sound pierced the stillness—a low, growling hum that vibrated through her bones. The darkness around her was alive, swirling and pulsing, its shadows moving like living creatures. Her body jerked violently as if she were being pulled in multiple directions at once, her muscles aching from the strain.

She tried to scream, but no sound escaped her lips. Her mouth was dry, her throat tight. Panic clawed at her chest, the desperate need to escape overwhelming her every thought. The cold deepened, an unnatural chill that seemed to seep into her very soul, freezing her from the inside out.

And then, suddenly, there was light. Not warmth, not comfort—just an unearthly glow, pale and sickly, that illuminated the endless black void around her. The light seemed to come from nowhere, but it was everywhere, casting long shadows that stretched and twisted as if they were alive.

Lily blinked, trying to make sense of what she was seeing. The space around her was vast, impossibly so. There was no sky, no stars, no ground beneath her feet—just infinite darkness stretching on all sides. And in the center of this void, there was something. Something that drew her in.

A shape. A figure. Or rather, a shadow of a figure.

It was standing just beyond the light, its outline flickering, its form shifting as if it were not entirely solid. The shape was tall, imposing, and though she could not make out its features, the sense of malice radiating from it was palpable. It wasn't human. It wasn't anything she could have ever imagined.

You shouldn't be here.

The voice echoed in her mind, though the figure had not moved, had not spoken a single word. It was the same voice she had heard before—the same cold, ancient whisper that chilled her to the bone.

Lily's heart raced in her chest, the sound of its pounding growing louder and louder in her ears. Her hands shook as she reached out, instinctively grasping for something—anything—to steady herself. The energy in the air was thick, oppressive, like a storm that was about to break.

The heart...

The word floated in her mind, chilling and familiar. The pendant around her neck pulsed in response, the heart inside it beating in sync with her own. But it wasn't just her heartbeat she felt. There was something else—something more primal, more ancient, thrumming beneath her skin.

It calls to you.

Her breath caught in her throat, a strangled gasp escaping her lips as the realization hit her. The heart inside her wasn't hers at all. It had never been hers. She was merely a vessel, a conduit, and it had been pulling her here all along.

The figure in the shadows moved. It was slow, deliberate, its steps heavy and unnatural, like something made of stone, grinding against the earth. But there was no earth. There was nothing here but the oppressive, suffocating darkness and that horrible, unending hum. Yet the figure's presence was growing closer, its shape more distinct, its details sharpening.

Lily forced herself to take a step back, her legs weak beneath her, her breath coming in sharp, panicked gasps. The figure's eyes— if they could be called eyes—glowed with a sickly, otherworldly light. They were not human eyes, nor any eyes she had ever seen, but something far older, something that made her feel as though she were nothing more than a fragile, fleeting thought in the universe.

She wanted to look away, to run, to hide. But she couldn't move. Her feet were glued to the cold, invisible ground, and the figure was so close now, so close that she could feel the weight of its gaze pressing down on her.

And then, with a sound like the cracking of stone, the figure spoke.

"You have come too far, Lily."

The voice was even colder than before, each word like an icicle piercing through the air. It felt like it was coming from all around her, reverberating in her bones, in her very soul.

"You think you are the key."

Lily's breath caught in her throat. The voice—this voice—came from somewhere deep within her, as though it was speaking directly to the heart, to the pendant around her neck. It knew her, knew everything about her. It knew the fear, the confusion, the desperation that had brought her here.

"You are not the key, Lily."

The words shattered the silence like a thunderclap, and the figure moved again. This time, it wasn't slow. It lunged toward her with terrifying speed, its long, elongated hands reaching for her throat.

She gasped, stepping backward, her pulse hammering in her ears as she tried to flee. But the void pressed in around her, the darkness shifting and writhing like a living thing, trapping her in its grip.

The figure's hands brushed against her skin, cold and unyielding. She gasped in terror, the sensation of being touched by something so ancient and malevolent overwhelming her. She could feel its cold breath against her face, the stench of decay and death wafting through the air.

"You cannot escape. You belong to the heart now."

Lily's mind reeled. The heart—it wasn't just a thing. It wasn't just some relic of an ancient past. It was alive. And it had chosen her.

The realization hit her like a wave, crashing over her with a force that stole her breath. She wasn't just its vessel. She was its prisoner.

Her hand went to the pendant again, her fingers trembling as she grasped it. The warmth of the heart inside had faded, replaced by something colder, something darker. The heart pulsed with an unnatural rhythm, pulling her toward the figure, pulling her toward whatever this thing was.

It wasn't just a shadow—it was part of the heart. The very essence of the heart. And it was claiming her now, drawing her into its grasp.

The figure's face—if it could be called a face—split open, revealing a mouth filled with jagged teeth that dripped with some black, oily substance. It grinned, a grin that stretched impossibly wide, showing her just how long it had been waiting.

Lily's legs buckled beneath her, her body crumbling under the weight of the fear, the understanding that there was no escape. She reached for the heart, clutching it with all her strength, but the darkness closed in, swallowing her whole.

"You are mine now."

The words echoed through her mind, and just as the darkness reached out to claim her completely, the world went black.

And then there was nothing.

# 12

## The Breaking Point

Lily's mind surged back to consciousness with a jarring force, like being ripped from a dream she didn't want to wake up from. She gasped for air, her chest heaving as though she had been underwater for far too long. The cold, the suffocating darkness—was it still there? Her pulse was pounding in her throat, her hands shaking violently as she tried to move, to rise, but her body felt heavy, as if it were submerged in the very air itself.

Slowly, her eyes fluttered open, the world around her still a swirling blur. The harsh, sickly glow she had seen earlier was gone, replaced by an oppressive dimness, the kind that seemed to suck the warmth from the very air. She was lying on something soft, yet cold, her back against what felt like stone. The faintest sound of distant dripping water echoed in the stillness, and she could taste the metallic tang of blood in the back of her throat.

Her hands shot to her neck instinctively, but there was no

pressure, no sign of the fingers that had once reached for her, intent on crushing her life away. No figure. No shadow.

Was it over?

Her thoughts collided in a frenzy, but one feeling stood out above the rest: dread. The air around her was suffused with it, thick and suffocating, like a living thing crawling under her skin, whispering words she didn't want to hear.

A movement—a shadow flitted across her vision.

Lily's head snapped up. Her breath froze in her chest. The shadow moved again, long and sinuous, its shape flickering in and out of the faint light like something not entirely real. She tensed, every nerve on high alert. She wasn't alone. The figure, whatever it was, was close—too close. And it was watching her.

Her heart thudded against her ribs, the rhythm erratic, frantic. She forced herself to rise, her limbs uncooperative, shaking with the shock of whatever had happened to her. She was in a place... somewhere cold, underground. The stone beneath her was slick with moisture, the air thick with a damp, rotten scent. The walls stretched up into the darkness, too high to see, and a low, grating hum filled the space, reverberating through the ground, vibrating in her very bones.

A sudden jolt of pain surged through her head, sharp and immediate, pulling her attention back to the present. Her fingers instinctively went to the pendant at her neck. The heart inside it pulsed, cold and insistent, like a heartbeat that wasn't her own. It was a steady, rhythmic thrum—unnaturally fast, as if something inside her was pushing her forward.

"Lily…"

The voice—her name—came from everywhere and nowhere at once, a whisper woven into the air itself. Her body went rigid, the hairs on the back of her neck standing on end. She turned in every direction, but the source of the voice remained hidden in the shadows.

"Lily, you cannot escape."

The voice, low and hoarse, slithered around her, inside her, each word filled with a power that made her bones ache. She couldn't see the figure yet, but she could feel its presence, the way it pressed against her skin, an invisible force squeezing the very air from her lungs.

A sudden movement caught her eye—this time, a figure more defined, more solid than before. It was tall, towering, its limbs stretched unnaturally long, dragging like dead weight behind it. Its face—or rather, its lack of face—was a blank, hollow void, the absence of something that should have been there. The darkness swirling around it seemed to pulse in rhythm with her own heartbeat.

The figure's presence radiated an unsettling, predatory energy, one that made her stomach twist in knots. It was not the same as the one from before—this one felt older, more malevolent, a thing of shadows that moved with purpose, and its every step seemed to bring it closer to her.

Lily's breath came quicker, the pressure in the air around her thickening, suffocating. She wanted to move, to run, but her legs refused to obey, locked in place by an unseen force. The darkness felt alive now, wrapping around her like chains, cold and tightening with every breath.

"You are here because you are meant to be."

The voice had a strange clarity now, and she realized it was coming from the figure itself, or rather, from deep within its emptiness. It wasn't speaking to her in words—its very presence was a command, its intention clear as it bore down on her, making her bones ache and her thoughts scatter.

Lily's fingers tightened around the pendant once more, her breath coming in shallow gasps as the realization set in. She had been led here. This wasn't an accident, not a chance encounter. The heart inside her had brought her here, to this place, to this moment.

But to what end?

The figure took another step forward, and this time, Lily felt the ground tremble beneath her, the walls groaning, as though the very cavern itself were alive and waking up. It was drawing closer, its shape solidifying, its presence too immense to ignore now.

I have to move, she thought frantically, but still, her legs refused to cooperate.

"You cannot fight this, Lily."

The voice was inside her mind now, invading her thoughts, lacing them with an icy dread that locked her in place. It was as though her very soul had been shackled by the figure's will. The darkness pressed in, wrapping around her like a cloak, pulling her into the cold embrace of the void.

A faint crackling sound broke through the silence—the soft, rhythmic hum of energy building, growing stronger, louder. The pendant burned against her chest, the heart inside it thumping erratically as if it were responding to the unseen force before her.

And then, in a moment of sheer terror, the air around her shifted.

The very fabric of reality seemed to bend, the shadows warping and twisting like smoke. The figure's outline began to dissolve, flickering, becoming nothing more than a ripple in the fabric of the world around her. But the darkness did not fade. No, the darkness only grew.

She felt the ground under her feet crack, and with it, a deep, primal rumble reverberated through her, shaking her to the core. Something was happening. Something beyond her control. Something that had been set into motion long before she had ever stepped foot in this forsaken place.

The darkness began to bleed into her very thoughts, flooding her mind with images, with sensations, with whispers she couldn't quite grasp. It was a force—no, a presence—that had been waiting for her. And now, it had found her.

Lily staggered backward, her vision swimming as the shadows coiled tighter, suffocating her. The whispers were louder now, every voice, every echo pressing in on her consciousness, until they merged into a single, unified scream:

"The heart is yours, Lily. You are ours."

Her mind shattered in that moment—the walls of her sanity cracking under the weight of the ancient force that had been lying in wait. The pendant burned against her skin, hotter, sharper now, the heart inside it pulsing wildly as it reached out for her.

And then, as if the world had had enough of the struggle, it broke.

A violent pulse shot through her chest, a jolt of energy that tore through her body and mind in a single moment of unbearable intensity.

And Lily fell into the darkness, her scream swallowed whole by the hollow heart that had claimed her.

# 13

# The Unraveling

Lily's eyes snapped open, her heart hammering in her chest as she gasped for breath. But this time, the air was different. Thick and oppressive, it hung in the space around her like a living thing, suffocating her. She could feel it pressing down on her chest, restricting her lungs. There was no escape.

For a moment, her vision was a blur, the edges of her sight distorted, swirling with dark, shifting shapes. She reached out, her fingers trembling as they grazed across cold, stone walls. The world around her seemed to pulse with a rhythm that wasn't hers. The heart—the heart—was beating, the same as it had before. Inside her. Against her will.

A sickly, eerie glow filled the space, casting jagged shadows across the walls. It was neither warm nor welcoming—just a strange, unnatural light that painted everything in hues of green and violet. The floor beneath her feet was slick with moisture, the cold seeping up into her bones, making her shiver uncontrollably.

Where was she?

Lily's mind struggled to grasp her surroundings. There were no doors, no windows—nothing that could tell her where she was, or why she was here. It felt like being trapped inside a tomb, buried under layers of rock and forgotten time. The air smelled of decay and something sharper, like iron. The deeper she breathed, the more she felt as though the walls themselves were closing in around her, pressing her into a space too small to move.

But then she heard it. A low, distant murmur, like a chorus of voices, faint but growing louder. A language she didn't recognize, yet felt strangely familiar. It wasn't human. It was as if the very earth was speaking, calling out to her.

She stumbled backward, the darkness closing in around her, pressing harder. Her breath quickened in panic as she tried to move, tried to escape, but the weight of the air was unbearable. Her legs trembled with the effort to stand, and the thudding in her chest grew louder, more erratic.

The voices swelled, filling her mind now, whispering things she couldn't understand but felt deep in her core. The words were alive, like insects crawling under her skin, scratching and biting, gnawing at her thoughts. She pressed her hands to her ears, but the voices only grew louder, louder, until they were no longer whispers but screams.

Lily.

The sound of her name cut through the chaos, and she froze, her body going rigid as the cold stone beneath her seemed to tremble. The voice—deep, rich, and ancient—spoke again, the power behind it so raw, so suffocating that it felt like it was tearing through her very soul.

You are not meant to be here.

It wasn't a question. It wasn't even a command. It was a truth, one that resonated deep within her, as though the earth itself had written it in the blood of ancient ones. The heart in her chest pounded in response, its beat frantic, insistent, urging her to act.

But act how? What could she do?

She spun around, her eyes scanning the darkness, searching for something—anything—that might explain what was happening. There had to be an answer. There had to be a way out.

Her hand reached instinctively for the pendant around her neck, her fingers brushing the smooth surface, the heart burning against her skin. She yanked it from her chest, but the weight of it felt heavier than before, dragging her down, pressing into her palm with an intensity that made her flinch. The light that had been pulsing inside the pendant was now dim, but somehow it seemed... wrong. Twisted. As if it were trying to pull her into its depths, swallowing her very essence.

She gripped it tighter, determined to tear it from her neck, to free herself from its grasp. But when she tried to pull it away, the pendant refused to move. It clung to her like an anchor, its power suffocating her.

A sound—sharp, guttural—cut through the air. It was behind her, too close, too real. Lily spun around, her breath catching in her throat as she came face to face with the figure.

The darkness swirled around it, cloaking its form in shadows, but she could still see it—feel it—just as she had before. The same eyes, glowing faintly in the dark. The same towering presence, its shape flickering between dimensions, between worlds. It was watching her with an intensity that made her stomach drop, its form flickering like a flame, dangerous and alive.

But this time, there was something different about it. Something more.

It reached out—a single, elongated hand—and as it did, Lily felt the ground tremble beneath her feet. The sound of cracking stone echoed through the chamber, and the walls around her seemed to ripple, as if the very reality she stood in was beginning to unravel. She tried to move, but the air had thickened, become viscous, like trying to push through tar. Her movements were slow, sluggish, and the figure's hand stretched toward her with agonizing slowness.

It was coming for her.

Her breath hitched as she backed away, desperate to put distance between herself and the encroaching presence. But no matter how far she moved, it seemed to stay right on her heels, the shadows growing deeper, more sinister, until she could no longer see the edges of the room.

You cannot escape the heart.

The words reverberated through the walls, through her mind, and Lily felt her knees buckle beneath her. The pendant grew hot against her skin, its pulse now erratic, as if it were somehow pulling her toward the figure, forcing her to submit.

She gasped for air, clutching the pendant tightly, feeling the warmth spread into her chest. The figure loomed closer, its presence suffocating. She reached for the heart inside her, her fingers trembling as the pendant throbbed, responding to the darkness surrounding her. The voices in her head were no longer whispers; they were commands, shouting at her, telling her to embrace the truth, to accept the bond, to surrender to the ancient power that sought to consume her.

"Lily."

The figure's voice filled her head once again, louder this time, as if it were speaking directly to her mind. The sensation was unbearable, an explosion of sound and force that made her vision blur and her heart race.

You are a part of it now.

The world around her began to crack, breaking apart like fragile glass. The shadows curled around her, spiraling inwards, pulling her into the darkness. The floor beneath her feet shattered, and she fell, tumbling into the abyss, the sounds of the earth splitting and the darkness closing in around her, suffocating her, consuming her.

She screamed, her voice lost in the chaos, her body falling deeper and deeper, until all that remained was the crushing weight of the heart—the heart that was now hers, as much a part of her as her own soul.

And in that moment, as the darkness consumed her, Lily understood.

There was no escape. The heart had her. And it would never let her go.

# 14

# The Choice

Lily's body slammed against cold stone, the impact jarring her senses back to life with a sickening twist. She lay there for a moment, gasping, trying to make sense of the disorienting rush of images, sounds, and sensations. Her pulse hammered in her throat, her chest rising and falling in frantic bursts. But the cold—the bone-chilling cold—was a constant presence, seeping into her skin, making her feel like a stranger in her own body.

The ground was slick beneath her, wet and uneven. She pushed herself up, the jagged edges of the stone scraping her palms as she moved. Her eyes flickered around the space, heart racing at the oppressive darkness that swallowed everything in sight. Her breath hitched as she strained to see. Was she... Was she underground? In some sort of cave?

The walls, smooth and unyielding, stretched high above her, disappearing into shadows too deep to penetrate. The air around her was thick with the scent of damp earth and something else—a sharp, acrid tang that stung her nostrils.

But it wasn't the cold or the darkness that made her blood run cold. No, it was the feeling—that feeling. The air was heavy with something far worse than fear. It was a presence, one that she couldn't see, but that she could feel. The hairs on the back of her neck stood on end, the world around her rippling with energy she couldn't comprehend.

A pulse—her heart—thudded in her ears, louder than before. The pendant hung heavily around her neck, its once rhythmic beat now erratic and almost desperate, like something living, struggling against the chains that bound it to her.

It was as if the very room were alive, watching her. Waiting.

"Lily..." The whisper came again, barely audible, but it crawled into her mind like a slow poison. The voice was so soft, so distant, and yet its presence seemed to fill the entire cavern. She froze, her body locking in place as the realization slowly took hold.

It was inside her.

That was the truth. That was what the voices, the presence, the darkness—the heart—had been trying to tell her. It was never just about escaping. It had always been about accepting.

She jerked the pendant from her neck, her fingers trembling, the cold surface burning against her skin as though it were alive. She held it out in front of her, feeling its power surge against her palm, almost as if it were struggling to break free from her grip. It was a living thing—this heart inside of it. She had always known it on some level, but now she could feel its pulsing, desperate need to become.

The ground beneath her shuddered, a low groan vibrating through the stone like the prelude to something much darker. Lily's breath quickened, panic rising like bile in the back of her throat. It was happening again—the feeling of the world unravelling. Her heart pounded harder, the beat matching the rhythm of the tremors. Her fingers clenched tighter around the pendant as the shadows seemed to shift, twisting and swirling with an unnatural ferocity.

Something was coming. And it was drawing closer.

Her eyes darted across the room, searching for any sign of movement. There was nothing. Just the silence. The suffocating silence.

And then she felt it.

The air shifted, heavy and thick, as if a weight had descended on her shoulders. Something—no, someone—was there. Watching.

Lily spun around, her breath catching as she stared into the blackness. There, emerging from the shadows, was the figure. It moved with the smoothness of a predator, gliding across the room with a terrifying grace. The figure's form rippled, flickering in and out of the darkness, too fluid to be real. But the eyes—those eyes—those glowing eyes were unmistakable. They shone with an unnatural light, a sickly greenish hue that reflected in the dark void.

She froze, the world grinding to a halt. The figure stepped closer, and the air seemed to pulse with its every movement, each step a painful reminder of the power it held.

No escape, it whispered again. There is no escape from the choice.

The voice was the same as before, cold and deep, seeping into her very bones. Lily's body tensed as the figure loomed over her, its presence oppressive, suffocating. She tried to speak, to demand answers, but no words came.

The figure's hollow gaze seemed to pierce right through her, searching her soul. She could feel the weight of its gaze pressing into her, unraveling her thoughts, until there was nothing left but fear and the suffocating pull of the heart.

You know what must be done.

The figure raised a hand, long fingers stretching toward her like claws. But it wasn't the hand she feared—it was the look in its eyes. The figure wasn't just a creature of darkness; it was a part of her. It was the manifestation of something that had been waiting, lying dormant inside her, and now it was awake. Now it wanted to claim her completely.

You are a part of it now, the voice inside her mind whispered again.

Lily shook her head, her breath coming in shallow gasps as she stepped back. She could feel the power of the heart growing, pulsing in time with the figure's every movement. It was forcing her to listen, to submit, but she wouldn't. She couldn't.

The world began to shift again, the stone beneath her feet trembling as cracks spread across the walls. Her thoughts were chaotic now, a swirling vortex of doubt and terror. What was happening?

Her fingers tightened around the pendant, its weight growing heavier with each passing second. It was pulling her in, as if it were trying to fuse with her, consume her entirely. And yet, the whispers—the voices—were louder now, too loud, too close. They were telling her something else now.

A choice.

She had a choice.

Lily's mind reeled. The figure before her shifted again, its form rippling like smoke, its eyes burning with an ancient fire. It opened its mouth, but no words came. Only the crushing, oppressive presence of its hunger.

She understood now.

The heart, the pendant, the figure—it was all part of the same thing. And she was at the center of it. She was the one who held the power to destroy it or to unleash it fully upon the world. The choice was hers. To accept it. To embrace it. Or to break free.

A surge of cold fear gripped her chest, but something else stirred within her, deep in her core. The faintest glimmer of resistance, of defiance. She wasn't just a vessel. She wasn't a pawn in this dark game. She was the key.

Choose, Lily.

The figure's voice echoed around her, blending with the whispers of the heart, filling her with the weight of its command.

Her heart thundered in her chest, every beat a painful reminder of the power inside her, inside the pendant. She closed her eyes for a moment, fighting the rush of panic that threatened to consume her. And then, with trembling hands, she made her choice.

But she would not be the one to bow to the darkness.

The heart had wanted her. It had wanted to break her. But she would never let it win. Never.

Lily lifted her hands, pushing the pendant forward as a surge of energy shot through her, a wave of cold fire sweeping over her body. She could feel the power gathering, twisting, cracking, until the air around her hummed with it, electric and alive.

And then she broke.

The sound of the earth splitting was deafening, the light of the pendant blinding as it erupted in a pulse of raw energy, a storm of power that sent the figure stumbling backward, screeching in fury.

But Lily stood firm, the power coursing through her as the choice she had made began to unravel everything. The heart pulsed one final time—and then fell silent.

And in that moment, everything went dark.

# 15

# The Price of Power

Lily's eyes fluttered open to a silence so complete it felt unnatural, suffocating. She didn't know where she was, or how long it had been. Her head throbbed as though a thousand knives had pierced her skull, and her body was sore, as though she had been dragged across rough stone. The world around her was still, like the moment after a storm when the air hangs heavy with an unspoken threat.

She pushed herself up, a sharp pain jolting through her ribs as she sat. Her hands shook as she braced herself against the cold stone beneath her. The cave—the dark, oppressive space she had been in just moments ago—was gone. In its place was something different. Something worse.

The walls were now covered in strange, shifting symbols—glyphs that glowed faintly in the dark. They pulsed with an eerie rhythm, like the beating of a heart, only it wasn't hers. The air was thick, suffused with an ancient, malevolent energy that felt like it was closing in on her. It wasn't just oppressive;

it was alive.

Lily gasped for air, her breath coming in quick, shallow bursts. The pendant—the heart—was still around her neck, but it felt different now. Heavier. Like it had changed, somehow. She lifted it to her chest, and the warmth of it burned against her skin, like an iron brand searing through her flesh.

"No..." she whispered, clutching at the pendant, feeling it pulse in her hand as if it were trying to communicate with her, to make her listen. But Lily didn't want to listen. Not anymore.

The world around her seemed to waver, as if she were seeing through a veil. And then the shadows stirred. Slowly, creeping across the walls like smoke, they took shape. Figures. Dark, towering figures. They moved toward her in a way that made her skin crawl, their forms flickering in and out of existence. She couldn't see their faces—there were no features, no eyes, just darkness where their faces should have been. But she could feel them, their presence like cold hands pressing against her skin.

She opened her mouth to scream, but no sound came out. Her chest tightened, suffocating under the weight of the air, the weight of them. The shadows gathered around her, closing in, blocking out all light.

And then—it—the figure. The one that had been haunting her dreams, the one that had pushed her to the brink. It stepped forward from the darkness, its form flickering like a dying flame. Its eyes—those piercing, glowing eyes—stared at her, locking with hers in a silent battle of wills.

"You did it," the figure's voice rumbled, so deep it felt like it was coming from inside her own mind. "You chose."

Lily tried to back away, but there was nowhere to go. The walls were pressing in, the shadows, too, gathering in every corner, suffocating her with their weight. Her breath quickened, her heart pounding harder as the reality of what she had done—the power she had unleashed—sank in.

"You chose," the figure repeated, its voice growing darker. "Now you will pay the price."

The words echoed through her head, a mantra, a curse. She had thought she had gained control. She had thought she had shattered the chains, but the truth was more insidious than she could have imagined. She hadn't freed herself. She had bound herself to something far worse.

The shadows moved, surrounding her now, enclosing her in their suffocating grip. She felt the cold breath of the figure on her skin, its presence pressing down on her, seeping into her very soul. Her hands trembled as she clutched the pendant to her chest, the heart now burning with a furious heat.

"What have I done?" she whispered, her voice trembling.

"You freed it," the figure said, stepping closer, its form flickering like a dying star. "But now it owns you."

Lily's pulse thundered in her ears, her thoughts spiraling. *No. It can't be. I had to do it. I had to destroy it, break free.* But the words she spoke to herself felt hollow, empty, as if the choice she had made had been nothing more than a trap.

The walls seemed to close in further, the symbols on them shifting faster, their rhythm growing more frantic. The shadows laughed—a low, guttural sound that vibrated through the air, filling her with a terror she couldn't explain.

*There is no escape.*

The voice was not the figure's now. It was the pendant. It was the heart. It was inside her.

Her fingers dug into the pendant, as though trying to pull it from her neck, but the more she pulled, the tighter it seemed to cling. It was fused to her, its power now irrevocably a part of her being. The heart inside of it pulsed wildly, thrumming with a malevolent energy. The world around her seemed to bend, the shadows stretching and warping, coiling around her like serpents, tightening with each passing moment.

"What do you want from me?" Lily cried, her voice raw, pleading.

The figure moved closer, its form flickering more intensely now, as if the fabric of reality itself were beginning to tear. It stopped just before her, its presence towering over her, suffocating in its sheer power.

"You've freed the heart, but in doing so, you've bound yourself to it," the figure intoned, its voice dripping with cold amusement. "You thought you could control it, but the heart controls you. It feeds on your fear, your doubts, your very essence. And when it has consumed you completely, it will destroy you."

Lily's chest constricted. The heart. She could feel it now, more clearly than ever before. It was not just a part of her—it was her. And it wanted her to surrender. It wanted her to give in. To let go. But she couldn't. Not yet.

The shadows twisted around her, their forms shifting and warping, dancing in time with the heartbeat that echoed through the room. Her breath came in desperate gasps, her mind reeling as she tried to think, tried to find a way out. But the more she fought, the tighter the darkness held her.

"What—what is this?" she demanded, her voice trembling with fear and frustration.

The figure's lips curled into a smile, its features still obscured by the shadows. "This is your destiny. The heart cannot be separated from you. It is a part of you, and now... now you must decide whether you will embrace it or be consumed."

Lily's heart thudded painfully in her chest as the weight of the figure's words sank in. She hadn't been freed. She had been chosen. Chosen by the heart. Chosen to serve its will. She had wanted to break the cycle, to escape the darkness, but now she realized that there was no escaping it. There never had been.

## THE PRICE OF POWER

The power was hers, but it came with a price.

And that price was her soul.

The figure stepped back, fading into the shadows, leaving her alone with her thoughts, with the heart that now beat within her chest. She stood there, trembling, feeling the weight of the decision settle over her like a shroud. She had thought she had made a choice, but the truth was far more sinister. There was no way to escape it. The heart would claim her, and with it, her soul.

She felt the cold, empty space inside her fill with the power of the heart, pulsing in time with her own heartbeat. The darkness whispered to her, a voice too soft to hear, but loud enough to make her soul tremble.

And Lily knew, in that moment, that there was no turning back.

She was bound to the heart. Forever.

# 16

# The Reckoning

The air felt different—heavier, colder—as though the very atmosphere had thickened with the weight of some terrible truth. Lily's breath came in shallow, desperate gasps as she stared into the black void of the room. The shadows shifted, their forms becoming more defined with each passing moment, twisting and contorting in the corner of her vision. The darkness was no longer just a backdrop—it was alive. And so, too, was the heart.

Her heart.

The pulse within her chest echoed through her entire body, a thrum of power that wasn't just felt but sensed. It moved through her, weaving its way into her veins, suffusing her muscles with an unnatural energy. The pendant, now warm against her skin, seemed to hum with a life of its own. The warmth spread from her neck down through her arms, across her legs, until her entire body felt as though it were about to burst with power.

But it wasn't power she wanted. It was freedom.

The whispers came again, rising from the depths of her mind, soft and insidious, like a lover's caress. But it wasn't a lover—it was the heart. It was feeding on her fear, on her uncertainty. It was feeding on her very soul.

Let go, Lily. Embrace it. There is no escape now.

The words wrapped around her, drawing her deeper into the darkness. She shook her head, trying to block them out, but they continued to grow louder. The whispers turned into voices, and then into a cacophony of demands, each one more insistent than the last. The heart wanted her. Needed her. It wanted her to succumb, to yield to its will.

But she couldn't. She wouldn't.

"No," she whispered fiercely, her voice trembling as she gripped the pendant tighter. "I won't let you control me."

She stumbled back, her feet slipping against the slick stone floor, but the shadows followed. They twisted and stretched like creatures of the night, closing in around her, drawing her in with their cold embrace. She felt the darkness press against her skin, pushing her, forcing her to surrender. Every part of her screamed to break free, but the heart—her heart—was getting louder, its pulse rising like a storm.

"Lily..." The voice was all-encompassing now, filling her thoughts, drowning out everything else. It was no longer a whisper, but a growl, deep and primal, coming from all around her.

It's time. You've given yourself to it. You're mine.

Her stomach churned as her pulse quickened. She wanted to scream. She wanted to tear the pendant from her neck and destroy it. But she couldn't. It was as if her own hands betrayed her, her body no longer responding to her commands. The pendant burned hotter against her skin, sending waves of heat through her veins.

The room around her seemed to shift, bending and warping, until the walls began to close in. The shadows didn't just surround her anymore—they moved, flowing like liquid, slithering across the stone with malicious intent. The symbols on the walls began to glow brighter, their eerie light pulsing in time with the heart's beat, illuminating the space with an unnatural glow.

Her vision blurred as her mind struggled to hold on, to make sense of what was happening. It wasn't just the darkness. It wasn't just the whispers. The room itself seemed to be alive, closing in on her as though it were a living, breathing entity. And she—she was the sacrifice.

The figure emerged from the shadows again, this time far closer than before. Its form shifted and writhed in the dim light, flickering between one shape and another, but its eyes—those terrifying, glowing eyes—were unwavering, fixed solely on her.

"You're too weak to fight it, Lily," the figure crooned, its voice echoing in her mind. "You made a choice. You can't escape it. The heart is part of you now. You are part of it."

Her head swam with the weight of the figure's words. She had known. She had always known, deep down, that there would be no simple escape from the heart. But hearing it now, spoken with such certainty, made her knees go weak. Her breath hitched. Her chest tightened. There was no way out. The heart was part of her, and it was growing stronger by the second.

"No," she gasped, her voice cracking as she fell to her knees, clutching at the pendant in a futile attempt to pry it from her skin. Her fingers burned, the heat radiating from the pendant like fire. But she couldn't release it. She couldn't let go. The heart was inside her, intertwined with her very being. It had become a part of her existence.

And it was feeding on her. On her soul.

The shadows surged forward, reaching out with tendrils of darkness that curled around her arms and legs, pulling her deeper into their grasp. Lily fought against them, every muscle straining, but it was no use. They were too strong. The power of the heart was too strong. She could feel it now, a growing hunger, an insatiable desire to consume her entirely.

The walls were closing in faster now, the symbols on them spinning in a chaotic whirl of light and shadow. The air crackled with energy, and Lily could feel the room shifting, distorting. It was as though the very fabric of reality was tearing at the seams.

"You wanted to destroy it," the figure murmured, its voice filled with dark amusement. "But in the end, you've only given it more power. The heart is no longer a weapon. It is a god. And you, Lily, are its vessel."

The figure's form flickered, its shape changing like smoke, as it stepped forward. Lily's breath caught in her throat as it raised a hand toward her. She could feel the weight of its presence—the crushing, suffocating energy that radiated from it.

"You'll never be free."

The words rang in her ears as the figure reached out, its hand closing around the pendant. And in that moment, she felt it—the sharp, burning pain in her chest, where the heart now lived. It was like nothing she had ever experienced. A jagged, searing pain that twisted through her soul, spreading outward in waves of unbearable agony.

"No!" she cried, her voice breaking. "No!"

But the heart didn't care.

With one final, agonizing tug, the figure pulled the pendant from her neck, and Lily felt the last remnants of her control slip away. Her hands were cold. Her body went limp. She could feel the darkness swallowing her whole, drowning her in its power.

And then, just as the world seemed to fade to nothing, she heard

## THE RECKONING

the whisper again.

It's too late now.

The darkness consumed her.

# 17

# The Broken Bond

Lily's eyes snapped open, but the world she saw was not the one she remembered. The edges of her vision blurred, and the air seemed to hum with a strange resonance, almost like a tuning fork held too long. Her breath came in short, jagged bursts, but it wasn't the physical pain that had awoken her. No, it was something else—something far darker.

Her hands were trembling, but she couldn't feel them. Or rather, it felt as though they were no longer her hands. It was as if she were watching someone else's movements, disembodied and detached, as though her very soul had been pulled from her body. Her heart... her heart was silent now.

The pendant was gone.

The cold, empty space around her spread, like an ink stain on her consciousness. She could still feel the faintest echo of the power that had once pulsed within her—strong, relentless—but now it was distant, like a dying ember flickering in the wind. But there was no warmth. No connection. Just the hollow emptiness.

Lily's head spun as she tried to push herself up, but the ground beneath her was unyielding, slick with a wetness she couldn't identify. She looked around, disoriented. The room was dark, impossibly so, and yet she could sense its vastness, stretching on in all directions, a cavernous void that swallowed the light. There were no walls, no ceiling—just darkness. The kind of darkness that crawled under your skin and made your pulse race. A darkness that knew you. That wanted you.

And then the voices returned.

They were a thousand whispers, overlapping, rising like the tide. They filled her mind, the words indistinguishable at first, but then... then they coalesced, sharp and clear.

It's too late. You can't fight it. You belong to it now.

The words slithered under her skin, wrapping around her heart, squeezing, squeezing until her chest burned with the pressure. She gasped, her hands flying to her chest, as if she could force the suffocating grip of those voices out, but it was no use. The darkness had already taken root, digging its claws deep into her soul.

She couldn't feel the pendant anymore, but she could feel it in her mind. It wasn't gone. It wasn't just a thing—no, it was inside her, like a shadow that stretched across her very being. It pulsed, relentless, hungry. The whispers were its voice, its will, and it was always watching. Always waiting.

You cannot escape. You cannot outrun it.

Her breath hitched as she squeezed her eyes shut, trying to block it out, but the cold touch of the presence inside her grew stronger. The silence around her thickened, pressing in, making her feel small, insignificant. The deeper she sank into the void, the more suffocating the pressure became.

And then, as though the darkness had a mind of its own, something shifted.

A cold breeze stirred around her, making the dampness on her skin seem colder still. It felt like a presence moving just beyond the edges of her perception, something... or someone who had crossed into this realm. Her pulse quickened, and she instinctively reached for something—anything—her hands grasping at nothing.

And then, as if to answer her unspoken plea, the first flicker of light appeared in the distance. At first, it was so faint that she thought her mind was playing tricks on her. But then it grew, slowly—steadily—a pinpoint of light, bright and pure, cutting through the darkness like a blade.

Lily's breath caught in her throat. It was real. She wasn't imagining it.

The light moved toward her, pushing back the shadows as it came, and she dared not breathe as it approached. She didn't know what it was, but the hope it brought with it was like a lifeline thrown into an ocean. She reached for it, her hands trembling in the cold, trying to get closer.

But as the light neared, she saw the shape of it—a figure. Tall, cloaked in shadows of its own, moving with a grace that seemed unnatural. The edges of its form rippled like smoke, never fully solid, never fully still. But its eyes—its eyes—burned with a pale, eerie glow, locking onto hers.

Lily stopped moving.

For the first time, in a long while, she felt the pull of something outside of herself. Fear. The figure's eyes—those burning orbs—seemed to see into her, through her, laying bare every part of her soul. It wasn't human. It wasn't anything she could recognize. Its presence was otherworldly, impossibly ancient, like something that had existed long before the world as she knew it.

"You... You're the one," she whispered, her voice trembling, barely able to form the words.

The figure said nothing. It didn't need to.

Instead, the light that emanated from it flickered, and the shadows recoiled, writhing as if they were alive, desperate to stay close to Lily. The dark was trying to claw its way back to her, to swallow the light whole.

But the figure remained unfazed. It took another step toward her, its form solidifying as it drew closer. Every movement was fluid, like a dream. Like a force that bent reality itself.

And then, without warning, the figure extended a hand toward her.

Lily recoiled instinctively, her body frozen in fear. Something inside her—the heart, that wretched, corrupted thing—fought against it, a primal urge to resist.

"You can't help me," she whispered, the words coming out in a rasp. "I'm... I'm already lost."

The figure's hand hovered just before her face, and then it spoke—not with words, but with a voice that reverberated through her mind.

Not lost, child. But broken. And the bond... it is not yet severed.

The words echoed, curling into her mind, settling in her chest. Her heart, the very thing she had fought to free herself from, pulsed in answer, its echo deep and violent.

The figure's hand slowly, gently, touched her cheek. For a brief moment, it was warm—comforting even. And then the warmth vanished, leaving only cold, like the touch of the grave.

There is always a choice, Lily.

Her breath quickened. Her chest rose and fell rapidly as she tried to comprehend the meaning of those words. The shadows that had consumed her life, her very soul, were starting to pull back. The light from the figure burned brighter, pushing them away. But she could feel them. The darkness was never far. It was always there, tugging at the edges of her mind, coiling itself back into the cracks of her soul.

The figure's face—if it could be called a face—shifted. A shadowy, shifting mask of light and dark, with only its eyes visible, fixed and unblinking.

You cannot be freed without sacrifice.

The words rang in her mind. The bond was not broken, and perhaps it never would be. It was tied to her, to her very soul. But there was a choice—a sacrifice—but at what cost? Could she truly break free, or was she destined to serve the heart forever?

The light in the figure's eyes burned brighter.

And then Lily realized something: The darkness would never let her go. The heart, the power she had once thought was hers to control, was simply using her. The figure had not come to save her. It had come to give her a choice—one she wasn't ready to make. The darkness that filled her was the only thing that could see the heart for what it was.

And she could either succumb to it... or fight for the part of her that was still human.

The darkness still watched, but now, it was her turn to decide.

# 18

# A Thief in the Night

Lily's heart pounded erratically in her chest, the rhythmic thump of it echoing in her ears as the figure before her slowly began to retreat into the shadows. She could still feel the warmth of its presence, like the faintest breath on her neck, but it was fading. The bond—her connection to the darkness—remained, and she felt its claws still gripping her, pulling her in. The cold fingers of the heart tightened in her chest.

The room had shifted again, swirling and warping around her as if the very air itself was alive, but this time, she didn't feel lost. She felt a surge of something else—something she couldn't place. Hope? No. It was more like desperation. She wasn't sure who she was anymore. She wasn't sure where she ended and the darkness began.

And then, the whispering returned. The voices.

Don't listen to it. It can't help you. It can never help you.

The words were so familiar now, so much a part of her that they no longer made her tremble. She gripped her hands into fists, nails digging into her palms, trying to silence the whispers. It wasn't the heart. It wasn't the figure. It was her. She was the one holding herself back.

The shadows danced at the edges of her vision, just out of reach, and with each flicker of light, they grew stronger, more insistent. They didn't want her to leave, didn't want her to break free. The heart didn't just beat inside her. It ruled her now.

But as Lily took another unsteady step forward, she felt something—an eerie, unmistakable presence. She froze, her breath catching. It was as though she were being watched, but she wasn't alone. There was someone else in the room, a silhouette, barely visible but so close that she could feel its cold, prickling gaze.

A figure.

Her pulse quickened. The air felt dense, and she instinctively took another step, her eyes darting around, searching for the source. The shadows in the room were alive, moving, but this figure... this one was different. There was something familiar about it.

She didn't have time to think. Something—or someone—was here.

There was a soft click behind her. A sharp, barely audible noise that sent a jolt of terror up her spine. Her breath hitched, and without warning, she whirled around, her heart stopping in her chest as she faced the empty room. Nothing. Just shadows.

Her instincts screamed at her to run, but where? There was no door. No window. No way out. She was trapped.

Then, there was another sound—footsteps. Faint, measured, but unmistakably close.

Lily's heart thudded painfully in her chest as the footsteps grew louder, coming from the darkness. Her breath came in shallow gasps, her mind racing to make sense of what was happening. She turned, trying to spot the movement, her gaze darting across the darkened room, but nothing. The figure she'd seen before—the one that had glowed with an otherworldly light—was gone, leaving only an empty silence.

Don't panic, she told herself, her throat tight with fear. You're not alone in this.

She took another step back, her foot slipping on the slick stone beneath her. Her pulse hammered against her ribs as she twisted, trying to steady herself. Her eyes scanned every inch of the space, every shadow. The figure was there. She could feel it. Something was shifting, just beyond her reach, but it was there.

Her fingers tingled, a strange warmth creeping up her arms. The heart—it was responding. Something inside her stirred, like the stirring of a storm. But this time, she didn't want it.

This time, it was the last thing she wanted.

A figure emerged from the shadows, not like the one she had seen earlier. This one was smaller, its silhouette cloaked in black, its presence oddly silent, despite the fact that Lily could feel its weight pressing in on her. The figure's face was obscured by a hood, but she could feel its eyes on her—cold, unfeeling eyes that seemed to see through her very being.

It spoke, its voice low and measured, carrying the weight of something ancient and powerful.

"You shouldn't have come here."

Lily's breath hitched. She had no idea who—or what—this figure was, but there was something in its voice that sent a chill down her spine. It wasn't an enemy, at least not in the traditional sense. There was something familiar about it. Something wrong.

"Who are you?" she whispered, her voice barely audible.

The figure took a step closer, its cloak swirling like smoke in the dim light. For a moment, Lily thought she could see a glimpse of its face—a flash of pale skin beneath the hood, but it was gone too quickly for her to truly see.

The figure's laugh was soft, almost amused.

"Who am I? I should be asking you that question."

The room felt smaller, closing in around her. Every instinct told her to run, to fight, but her body refused to move. The shadows around her seemed to press closer with every word the figure spoke, as though they were hungry for something more—something she didn't understand.

She swallowed hard, struggling to keep her composure.

"What do you want from me?" Her voice was steadier than she felt.

The figure paused, its gaze never leaving her. The silence stretched, taut and painful.

"I came to take something from you. Something that belongs to me."

Lily's pulse quickened. "What?"

But the figure didn't answer immediately. Instead, it moved forward in a fluid, almost predatory motion, stepping closer until it was within arm's reach. It was then that Lily saw it—the glint of something sharp, something metallic, hidden beneath the folds of its cloak. Her throat tightened as she realized what it was.

A blade.

The figure reached out with one hand, its fingers long and thin, and Lily instinctively took a step back, her heart racing. The blade was a threat, but there was something else—something far more sinister. The figure wasn't here for a fight. It wasn't here to kill her.

It was here to steal something.

Lily's thoughts raced, but she couldn't seem to gather them in time. Before she could react, the figure's other hand shot out, gripping her arm with unrelenting force. The coldness of its touch seeped into her skin, and Lily gasped, trying to pull away. But it was useless. Its grip tightened, unyielding, and she could feel something cold, sharp, pressing against her throat.

"No," she gasped, her pulse pounding in her ears. "What do you want with me?"

The figure's lips curled into a smile, though the expression was more predatory than comforting.

"I want what's inside you, Lily. The heart."

Lily's heart skipped a beat. The heart. The very thing she'd been fighting against—the thing that had taken over her life.

"I won't give it to you," she said, her voice fierce, even as fear gnawed at her insides.

The figure's smile deepened. "You don't have a choice."

With a sudden, brutal movement, the figure yanked at her pendant, ripping it from her neck. Lily cried out, but there was no time for pain. The moment the pendant left her skin, she felt the room shift once again—the ground beneath her feet trembled, and the darkness seemed to writhe, alive and hungry.

The figure stepped back, holding the pendant aloft, and Lily felt a sharp pang in her chest—a physical ache, as if the pendant had been a part of her heart, and now it was gone.

The figure tilted its head, studying her with cold, calculating eyes. And then, in a voice that sent a jolt of terror through her veins, it whispered, "You've been a thief all along, Lily. But now, it's my turn to steal."

Lily's vision blurred as her world tilted into darkness once again.

# 19

# The Price of Power

Lily's world spun violently as the figure stepped back, the pendant clutched tightly in its hand. The cold metal seemed to hum with an almost malevolent energy, its sharp edges glinting under the faint light. She could feel it. The absence. The hollow space where the pendant had once been, like a part of her soul had been ripped away. Her breath came in ragged gasps as the world around her shifted, the air thick with a palpable sense of dread.

The shadows gathered, swirling with an unholy hunger, whispering louder now, their voices pressing against her consciousness. They wanted to swallow her whole. The heart. The power that had once been tethered to her, now seemed to have been torn away, leaving behind nothing but raw, exposed nerves.

She reached for her neck, but the pendant was gone, lost to the figure that stood before her, its cloak swirling like a dark storm. The figure's eyes burned with an intense, predatory hunger, and Lily could feel the pull of its gaze as though it were physically drawing her in. Every instinct screamed for her to move, to run, to fight, but her body refused to obey. It was as if she were trapped in a dream, frozen, unable to break free.

"You should have known better, Lily," the figure murmured, its voice like silk, cold and smooth. It sounded so familiar, and yet, she couldn't place it. "The heart is never truly yours. It was always meant to belong to me."

Lily shook her head, her vision swimming as she tried to steady herself. "No..." she whispered, her voice shaking with disbelief. "I won't let you have it."

The figure's lips curled into a thin, malicious smile. "You don't have a choice anymore."

Lily's hands clenched into fists at her sides, the anger rising in her chest like a flame that refused to be extinguished. She could still feel the remnants of the power inside her, faint but persistent, like a pulse beneath her skin. The heart was gone, but something else remained. She could feel it. Her.

"I won't let you take it," she said again, louder this time, her voice trembling with newfound defiance. The figure laughed softly, the sound echoing through the shadows, as though it were amused by her resistance.

"You've already lost, Lily," it said, its voice dripping with disdain. "The power you think you still hold—it's mine. It always has been. All this time, you were just a vessel. A pawn."

The air seemed to thicken, the shadows growing darker, suffocating, as if the room itself were closing in on her. She could hear the whispers more clearly now, louder and more urgent. Join us, Lily. Join us and feel the power surge. Let us consume you.

Her vision blurred, but there was no mistaking the figure's intent. It wasn't here to bargain. It wasn't here to negotiate. It had come to take. To take everything she had left, and leave her a hollow shell.

But the power inside her wasn't gone. No, it was still there, faint but flickering. Her pulse surged in time with it, and for the first time in what felt like forever, she felt a flicker of hope.

The pendant, the heart—it was more than just an object. It was her, a part of her. If the figure thought it could take it, it had underestimated the bond they shared.

"You're wrong," Lily said, her voice gaining strength with each word. "The heart was never yours to take. It never was."

The figure's smile faltered for a brief moment, but the coldness returned almost immediately. "You don't understand, do you? The heart has chosen. It's chosen me." It stepped forward, its hand outstretched, and Lily could feel the pull, the unnatural draw of its presence, as though it were physically siphoning the very essence from her.

But Lily refused to back down. She focused on the sensation, the pull, the flickering of power deep within her. She closed her eyes, drawing on the thread of light that remained in her chest, the last vestiges of the magic that had once coursed through her veins. It wasn't much, but it was enough. It had to be.

With a desperate cry, she reached out, stretching her hand toward the figure, her fingers crackling with the remnants of the energy she had fought to retain. The darkness recoiled, hesitant, but the figure did not waver. Instead, its grip on the pendant tightened, and with a single, fluid motion, it raised the heart high, the pendant gleaming like a knife in the dim light.

Lily's heart skipped a beat.

"No!" she cried, her voice hoarse and frantic. "You don't understand! The heart won't obey you!"

But the figure only smiled again, that cold, knowing smile that sent a shiver down her spine. "It already obeys me, Lily. It always has. The moment you gave it power, the moment you took it into your chest, you made the choice."

The room shifted again, the shadows twisting into shapes that seemed almost sentient. Lily could feel the walls closing in, the air thickening as the presence in the room became more oppressive, more consuming. The whispers turned to shrieks, their voices deafening as they crawled inside her mind, tearing at her thoughts, drowning out everything else.

You will submit. You will join us. You will be ours.

Her hands trembled, her knees buckling beneath her as the

weight of the darkness seemed to crush her, the pressure unbearable. Her chest burned with the coldness of the power being stolen from her. She was losing it. Losing herself.

No. She refused.

With the last ounce of strength she could muster, Lily drew in a sharp breath and focused on the one thing that still anchored her—the pulse within her heart. She could still feel it, faint but steady. It was the last piece of herself that remained.

Lily's voice broke through the din of the voices, shaking but filled with resolve. "I won't let you take it. You can't have me."

The figure's eyes narrowed, and it took a step closer, the air growing colder with each movement. "You have no choice, Lily. This is the price. The price of power."

And with that, the figure extended its hand once more, the heart glowing eerily in the darkness.

Lily's breath caught in her throat. For a single, terrifying moment, she was sure the heart would slip from her grasp, and the darkness would claim her forever.

But then, something inside her snapped.

With a guttural scream, Lily reached out, her fingers outstretched, and her voice a sharp cry of defiance. As her fingertips brushed against the pendant, a surge of raw, untapped energy shot through her, ripping through the shadows like a flame catching the wind.

The room erupted in a blinding flash of light.

For a moment, there was nothing. No sound. No movement. Only blinding, suffocating light.

When the light faded, the room had changed. The figure was gone, vanished as though it had never been. The shadows remained, but they no longer seemed to press in on her. The suffocating darkness had lifted, and Lily could breathe again.

But the power... the power was still there, deep within her, pulsing like a heart beat.

Lily sank to her knees, her head spinning, the weight of what had just happened settling over her. She had made a choice, but the cost was not yet clear. The heart was hers once again, but what had she lost in the process? What price had she paid for its return?

The shadows lingered around her, but she no longer felt their pull. The darkness was still there, still a part of her, but for the first time in a long while, she felt a spark of something she hadn't known she'd lost—freedom.

# 20

# The Return of the Dark

Lily's mind reeled as she slowly rose to her feet, her legs shaky, her body weak from the overwhelming force of the power that had surged through her. The room around her felt unreal, as if it were a dream—both familiar and alien at the same time. The shadows that had once been so oppressive now seemed still, like a quiet sea after a storm, yet the lingering sense of something dark and unseen was palpable. The air had shifted, heavy with an ominous tension that made her skin crawl.

She couldn't explain it—what had happened. The figure, the darkness, the heart—it was all tangled in her mind like a knot she couldn't undo. And now, standing in the middle of this quiet room, the silence felt louder than ever, echoing in the hollow spaces of her thoughts.

Had she truly won?

Her fingers instinctively reached for the pendant around her neck, her breath catching as she felt its weight against her skin once more. The heart was there. The cold, smooth surface of it pulsed beneath her touch, its power thrumming through her veins. It felt... different, somehow. More alive. But also more dangerous.

Lily's gaze darted around the room, but it was empty. The figure—the dark presence that had been so close, so insistent—was gone. The shadows had returned to their corners, harmless in their stillness. But she knew, deep down, that this wasn't over. The heart—her heart—had been claimed by the darkness before. It had chosen her once. But now... now, she wasn't so sure she could control it. She wasn't sure if she wanted to.

Her breath caught when she heard it—a soft whisper, like a breath in the dark. The sound came from the corner of the room, so faint that at first, she thought it was just her imagination. But then, the whisper grew louder, sharper, until it was impossible to ignore.

Lily... Lily...

The sound of her name, spoken in a low, hollow voice, sent a chill crawling up her spine. It wasn't her own voice—it wasn't even human. It was a whisper, a call from somewhere deep, from somewhere dark.

She spun around, her heart thudding in her chest, but there was no one there. The room was still.

What was that?

Lily took a cautious step forward, her breath shallow, her body tense. She was still reeling from the surge of power, and now, the room seemed to be closing in on her. The walls seemed to pulse with an energy of their own, the shadows twitching at the edges of her vision.

It's not over, she realized. The darkness had never truly left. It had just been waiting. Waiting for her to think she was safe.

Another whisper. Louder now, clearer. You can't escape me, Lily. You belong to me.

Lily's pulse quickened. The voice—cold, malevolent—seemed to be coming from all directions at once, as if the walls themselves were speaking to her. She pressed a hand to her forehead, trying to steady herself. She wasn't losing control again. She wouldn't.

But then the air around her began to thicken. The shadows seemed to twist, shifting, moving as if alive. They reached for her like long, clawed fingers, pulling at her skin, tugging at her very soul. She could feel them crawling beneath her clothes, seeping into her bones.

No!

She staggered back, the heat of the pendant searing against her chest. Her fingers dug into the metal, trying to ground herself, but the power, the dark pulse of the heart, was too strong. It was alive. It was growing.

Her breath caught in her throat when she saw them. Figures—shapes—emerged from the shadows. Tall, thin forms, their faces obscured by cloaks, their bodies twisted and unnatural. Their movements were jerky, like marionettes controlled by unseen strings. But their eyes... their eyes gleamed with hunger, with knowledge, and with a twisted, eerie intent.

Lily's heart pounded in her chest as the figures closed in on her. She wanted to run. She wanted to scream. But her feet were frozen to the floor, her body paralyzed by the pull of the darkness. It was as if they were a part of her, connected to the heart—her heart—that still burned with a cold fire in her chest.

"You can't hide," one of the figures spoke, its voice barely a whisper, barely human. But it carried weight, an ancient force that sent tremors through Lily's core. "The heart belongs to us, Lily. You cannot escape your destiny."

The words echoed in her mind, vibrating through her skull like a drumbeat. She had escaped once. She had fought to take control, to regain the power the heart had stolen from her. But now, the heart wasn't just hers—it was theirs too. They were part of it, just as she was. And they would take it from her, piece by piece, until there was nothing left.

The room darkened further as the figures stepped forward. Their faces remained hidden beneath their hoods, but Lily could feel their gaze, the weight of their presence bearing down on her, pressing her to the ground. It felt like she was drowning in the darkness, suffocating beneath its endless weight.

This isn't real, she thought desperately, fighting against the grip of fear that threatened to consume her. This is all in my head.

But as she turned to flee, her feet slipped beneath her, and the floor gave way. She fell, the darkness closing in like a tidal wave, its icy fingers reaching for her, pulling her deeper into the abyss.

Her thoughts raced, desperate for a way out. Think, Lily. Think!

Her hand shot to her chest, clutching the pendant, the only thing that still anchored her to this world. Her heart thudded in her chest, the rhythm of it frantic and erratic. The darkness twisted tighter, threatening to tear her apart, to consume her. But Lily refused to let go. She wouldn't lose herself again.

With a final, guttural scream, she threw herself forward, tearing herself away from the shadows, from the figures that hovered like specters at the edges of her vision. She couldn't let them take her. She couldn't let them win.

But the room wouldn't let her go. It bent, warped, and twisted around her. The shadows were no longer just shadows. They were real—tangible, alive. They pressed in from every direction, clawing at her, tugging at her, trying to pull her under.

And then she heard it. A voice, louder than the rest, deeper, more guttural.

You can't run, Lily.

It was the voice of the heart itself, and for the first time, she realized the full weight of her mistake. It wasn't just the figure, or the darkness—it was her.

The heart had never belonged to her. It was always meant for this.

A cold laugh echoed through the room, vibrating the very air. And in that moment, Lily understood.

It wasn't over. It was only just beginning.

# 21

## The Echoes of Fate

*Lily's breath came in ragged gasps as she stumbled backward, the weight of the darkness pressing down on her like a thousand invisible hands. She was no longer alone in the room; the shadows had taken on form, twisting into shapes that seemed almost human, their movements jerky and unnatural. Her pulse thundered in her ears as she tried to steady herself, her hand still clutching the pendant against her chest, as if its cold weight could protect her from the suffocating dread closing in from all sides.*

The figures were watching her, their faces obscured by the depths of their cloaks. They stood motionless at first, as though waiting, letting the silence stretch between them, thick and unnerving. Lily's eyes darted between them, her heart pounding in her throat. She couldn't shake the feeling that they were watching her with more than just their eyes—they were *inside* her, pulling at her very essence, their intent as clear as it was terrifying.

"You thought you could hide from us," one of the figures whispered, its voice like the rasp of dead leaves skittering across the ground. The words slid through the air, each syllable an accusation. "You thought you could escape your fate."

Lily's fingers tightened around the pendant, the cold surface biting into her skin. *Escape?* Had she truly thought she could escape the power that had always been with her? The heart, the darkness, had always been intertwined with her, even before she'd truly understood it.

She couldn't breathe. The air had become thick with the stench of decay, the walls pressing inward as if the very room was alive, twisting, hungry. Every inch of space felt as though it were closing in on her, suffocating her with the weight of what she had failed to understand. The shadows moved closer, now sliding along the floor, crawling up the walls, as though they had no true form, no true boundaries.

"Why did you think you could fight us, child?" the figure spoke again, its voice curling around her like a noose. "You belong to us. You always have."

Lily's vision blurred, her head spinning, and for a moment, she thought she might faint. She felt dizzy, the overwhelming force of their presence like a wave crashing over her. But through the haze, one thought emerged, clearer than the rest.

*I won't let them take me. Not again.*

With every ounce of will she had left, Lily straightened, her eyes narrowing as she faced the figures. She wasn't the same person who had been dragged into the darkness all those months ago. The heart—*her* heart—still pulsed beneath her skin, steady and strong, a reminder that it was still hers, despite everything. Despite them.

"Leave me be," Lily forced through clenched teeth, her voice shaking but defiant.

The shadows twisted, converging on her in an instant, their forms melting together like liquid night. She could feel the weight of them, the cold press of their power pushing against her, trying to crush her. But the pendant—her heart—burned brighter, stronger, as though it were calling to her, urging her to rise, to fight. The darkness recoiled for just a moment, as if uncertain, before surging forward again with renewed force.

Lily gasped, stumbling back, but the shadows were quicker. They wrapped around her arms, her legs, pulling her toward them with terrifying speed. She could hear them—voices, whispers, an unending chorus of *no* and *you belong to us* and *you cannot escape*—filling her ears, deafening her.

Her body burned. The pendant dug into her chest, but she could feel it now—an electric pulse, hotter than before, pushing back against the darkness. The bond was *there*. It had always been there. Her heart, the heart of the witch, the power of the darkness was hers to command. She wasn't just a vessel for it. She *was* the heart.

Lily's body trembled with the effort, but she raised her hands, pressing them against the floor as she concentrated on the pulse within her, on the thrum of the heart that was both a part of her and so much more. The shadows recoiled at the touch of her hands, as though the very air had changed. She could feel the power swirling inside her, hungry and untamed.

She closed her eyes, focusing. The darkness pressed in on her, but now, she could see it for what it truly was: a void, an endless chasm of need and hunger. The whispers were louder now, demanding, pleading for her to surrender. But Lily was no longer afraid of the shadows. She understood them.

She was the one who held the power.

Her heart surged. The pendant pulsed with a violent light, bright as a star, as the power inside her broke free. The shadows screamed, an awful, deafening noise that filled her head with an unbearable pressure, but she held firm, her hands steady as she directed the power outward.

The darkness faltered, and then—exploded.

It was like a great shockwave, a wave of light so blinding that it left nothing but emptiness in its wake. The walls of the room shook, the air humming with an energy so pure and raw it felt as though the very fabric of reality was being torn apart. Lily gasped for breath, her body shaking, but she stood tall, her fists clenched at her sides, her heart still burning fiercely within her.

And then, as quickly as it had come, the chaos stopped.

The shadows were gone. The figures had vanished, reduced to wisps of smoke that disappeared into the air. The room was still again, but now, it was different. The oppressive weight had lifted, replaced by an eerie calm that filled the space with a haunting silence.

Lily's chest rose and fell with every labored breath as she tried to steady herself, her hands trembling as she wiped the sweat from her brow. She had done it—she had fought them off. She had *won*. But as the last remnants of the darkness faded away, a cold realization settled in her gut.

This wasn't the end.

The heart still burned within her chest, and with it, something darker—something deeper than she had ever imagined. It had been hers, yes. But now, it was a part of her in ways she hadn't fully understood before. And with it came a price. The shadows would return. The hunger would never truly be sated.

Lily had won the battle. But the war was just beginning.

She knew, as surely as she knew her own name, that the darkness would find a way back. And when it did, she would be ready. Because this time, she wasn't just running. She wasn't just fighting.

She was the heart.

And it had already chosen her.

# 22

## The Depths of the Heart

The silence was suffocating, wrapping itself around Lily like a shroud, pressing her into the very floor she stood upon. She hadn't moved since the dark figures had disappeared, their ghostly whispers still echoing faintly in her ears, the sound of their departure lingering like smoke. Her breath was shallow, her pulse erratic, as she stood in the empty room, the pendant at her chest pulsing softly—a rhythmic beat that was both comforting and unnerving.

Lily's mind was reeling, still struggling to comprehend the depth of the power she now possessed, the power that had been forced upon her so many months ago. It was inescapable. It was a part of her. But something was wrong.

The shadows had left for now, but she could feel them, the tendrils of darkness twisting beneath her skin, waiting. Watching. Hungry. She could almost hear their voices, low and insistent, whispering in the corners of her mind, trying to break through the cracks in her consciousness.

The heart, the pendant—the source of all this power—was still there, cold and unyielding against her chest. But now, its pulse felt different, more insistent, more alive. It was as if it were calling to her, reaching out, urging her to surrender once again to its depths.

Lily shook her head, her hand pressing harder against the pendant as though it could somehow silence the voice. But it wouldn't go away.

The darkness had always been a part of her, even before the heart had chosen her. It had seeped into her life in subtle ways, in the moments she hadn't understood, in the shadows that had always seemed to move just out of the corner of her eye. But now... now it was real. The power was real. The hunger was real. And with each passing moment, the darkness that had once seemed so distant, so separate from her, was slowly becoming something she could no longer ignore.

Her vision blurred as a wave of dizziness swept over her. She swayed on her feet, her mind spinning as her legs threatened to give way beneath her. She gripped the edge of a nearby table to steady herself, the wood cold under her fingers, grounding her in a way that felt almost desperate.

I can't fall apart now. Not now.

A soft click echoed through the room, faint at first, but growing louder, reverberating off the walls. Her head snapped up, eyes wide, as the sound grew in intensity, until it was unmistakable. Someone—something—was at the door.

Lily's pulse quickened. She turned toward the door, her mind racing with possibilities, her heart pounding in her chest. She knew better than to think the darkness had truly gone. It had only retreated, waiting for the right moment to strike again. But who was there, at the door, now?

Another click, and the door creaked open.

Lily's breath caught as a figure stepped into the room. The air seemed to shift with their arrival, thick with an unfamiliar energy, the shadows tightening in their wake. The figure was tall, their face obscured by the low light, their presence heavy in the space. They moved slowly, deliberately, as if they knew that every step they took was a challenge to the fragile calm Lily had managed to cling to.

"You're still here," the figure said, their voice low, velvety, like a whisper from the dark itself. "I thought you'd have run by now."

Lily's hand instinctively tightened around the pendant, her heart racing, though she stood her ground. She tried to push back the rising tide of fear, but it clawed at her, threatening to drown her.

"Who are you?" she demanded, her voice barely a whisper, trembling with the weight of her own uncertainty. "What do you want from me?"

The figure stepped further into the room, and Lily's breath caught. It was not a stranger. She would have recognized that energy anywhere. The same darkness that had claimed her heart—its tendrils reached out, familiar, binding them. It was him.

The man from her past.

"You still don't understand," he said, the words laced with a quiet, dangerous amusement. "The heart doesn't just choose anyone. It chooses those who are meant to carry it. It chooses those who are worthy."

Lily felt a chill run through her, the words like ice in her veins. The room seemed to close in on her, the walls bending inward as if they, too, were aware of what was happening. She could feel the darkness shifting again, as if the air itself was alive with it.

"You didn't have a choice," the man continued, his voice softening, almost tender. "Not really. You were born to carry that heart. To hold it, to protect it, to let it grow inside of you."

Lily shook her head, her breath ragged. "No," she said, her voice firm. "I never asked for this. I never wanted this power."

A smile flickered at the corners of the man's lips. He stepped closer, his presence overwhelming, suffocating. She could feel the darkness wrapping itself around her once more, pulling at her. But this time, there was something more—a pulse, a pressure, as though the heart itself was reacting to his presence, pulling her toward him.

"You misunderstand, Lily," he said, his tone almost soothing. "You're not meant to resist it. You can't resist it. The heart calls to you because it is you. All the power you've felt, all the darkness you've fought... it's a part of you now. And the sooner you accept that, the easier this will be for you."

Lily's knees felt weak, her breath shallow, as the man's words sank into her mind, taking root in her thoughts. She wanted to resist, to scream, but the power of his voice was too strong, the weight of his presence too oppressive. She could feel herself teetering on the edge of something she didn't want to understand, something she was terrified of becoming.

"I'm not like you," Lily whispered, though she wasn't sure if it was a plea or a defiant statement. "I'm not like them."

The man's eyes glinted in the dim light, his gaze sharp and knowing. "No, you're not like them. You're something much greater."

The room seemed to pulse, the shadows gathering at the edges like dark, hungry creatures, waiting for their moment to strike. The man's words were not just spoken—they were felt, deep in Lily's chest, in the very core of her being.

You belong to it.

Her heart surged painfully, the rhythm in her chest quickening, each beat a reminder of the power she could no longer deny. She could feel the pull, the hunger of the heart reaching out for him, for the darkness that was still, always a part of her.

"You're wrong," she whispered through gritted teeth, forcing herself to stand tall, though her body trembled. "I'll never be like you."

The man's smile widened, but there was no kindness in it—only a cold, predatory amusement. He stepped closer, his fingers brushing against the pendant, sending a shock of icy power through her body.

"You don't have a choice," he said, his voice low, almost regretful. "But don't worry, Lily. You'll understand soon enough."

And with that, the room plunged into darkness. The shadows closed in around her, thick and impenetrable, and Lily felt the power of the heart surge through her, demanding, insisting, as the man's presence vanished into the void. The darkness had taken root in her once again.

But this time... this time, Lily wasn't sure if she could fight it.

The echoes of fate had already begun to reverberate in the depths of her heart.

# 23

## The Silent Promise

Lily's hands shook as she reached for the door, her mind a swirling mass of confusion and dread. The figure—the man—was gone, but his presence lingered like a dark cloud, choking the very air around her. The shadows, too, remained, moving in the corners of the room, their restless energy crawling along the walls like something alive. Every part of her wanted to run, to escape, but the weight of the heart, pulsing steadily against her chest, made that impossible. It held her in place, just as it had since the moment it had been forced into her life.

She had thought she could control it. She had believed, for a brief, fleeting moment, that she could keep the darkness at bay. But now, in the silence that followed the man's departure, Lily understood the truth with brutal clarity.

The heart was never hers to control.

With a heavy breath, she turned away from the door, her footsteps reluctant as she moved back into the center of the room. The weight of the pendant seemed to increase with each passing moment, its pulse a constant reminder of what was now a part of her, what could never be undone.

The darkness crept closer, the shadows thickening, pressing in around her like a wall. She could feel it now—them—waiting, their whispers a constant hum at the edges of her mind, urging her to surrender, to give in to the power she could no longer deny.

But she couldn't. Not like this. Not after everything she had fought for.

Her hand moved instinctively to the pendant again, fingers brushing the cold metal, the sharp edges biting into her skin. The power it contained was still there, the magic old and ancient, a force beyond her comprehension. It was no longer just a part of her life—it was her. It had always been her.

Lily swallowed hard, a bead of sweat sliding down her temple as the room seemed to pulse with an energy she couldn't control. The shadows, the voices, they were all growing louder, more insistent. She could feel the darkness calling her name, feel the tendrils of its power reaching for her, trying to pull her in.

"Enough," she whispered to the air, though her voice trembled with fear. "I won't let you take me."

But the shadows only thickened in response, wrapping around her, pressing in from all sides. There was no escape. No hiding.

The heart began to burn again, a searing heat that spread through her chest, its pulse erratic and frantic, as if it were alive, as if it were struggling to break free from her body. The more she tried to resist, the stronger it became, pushing against her, demanding to be let loose.

Suddenly, the pendant pulsed violently, a sharp jolt of power that sent Lily reeling back, her legs buckling beneath her. She collapsed to the floor, gasping for air, her hand clutching at her chest as though she could stop the pain, as though she could suppress the beating of the heart within her.

But it wouldn't stop.

The pain intensified, shooting through her veins like fire, each beat of the heart feeling as though it were tearing her apart from the inside. Her vision blurred, and she could feel her body trembling uncontrollably, the air around her growing thick with an oppressive, choking heat. She knew what was happening.

The heart was awakening.

It had always been waiting for this moment, for the right time to take control. She had known it deep down, but she had refused to see the truth. The heart wasn't just power—it was corruption. It wasn't meant to be wielded by anyone. It was a force of destruction, a force that could destroy everything and everyone it touched.

Lily gasped for air, her chest tightening as the pain became unbearable. Her fingers clenched around the pendant, but instead of fighting it, instead of trying to push it away, something inside her shifted. She had no choice.

She could feel it now, the dark pulse of the heart, reverberating deep inside her, melding with her own pulse, becoming one with her. It was inescapable. It was her. And the thought that she could fight it—that she could win—seemed laughable now.

Lily closed her eyes, a single tear slipping down her cheek as she whispered into the stillness, "I can't fight you anymore."

And as if responding to her surrender, the darkness surged. It swept through the room in a violent rush, enveloping her, drowning her in its cold embrace. She felt herself being pulled under, sinking into the void as the heart within her beat with relentless, unforgiving power.

The shadows wrapped themselves around her, intertwining with the threads of her thoughts, her soul. She could no longer distinguish where she ended and they began. There was no more Lily. Only the heart. Only the power. Only the darkness.

But even as the shadows consumed her, she heard the whisper again—clearer this time. Louder. More insistent.

"You were always meant for this, Lily. You always knew."

Her breath hitched, and she realized, with a sinking sense of horror, that the voice wasn't just in her head. It was real. It was here.

The man.

He was back.

The darkness pulsed again, pulling her deeper into the abyss, but this time, Lily didn't fight. She didn't resist. She didn't try to tear herself free. The heart—her heart—had finally claimed her. And in the depths of that cold, suffocating void, she could feel something else stirring, a dark promise that seemed to rise from the very core of the power that had consumed her.

It was the promise of destruction.

The promise of something far worse than anything she could have imagined.

And in that moment, as the darkness fully enveloped her, Lily understood the true nature of the heart. It wasn't a gift. It wasn't power. It was a curse.

One that she could never escape.

# 24

# The Unraveling

The air was thick with an unnatural chill, as if the world itself had frozen in time. Lily's every breath felt like it could shatter the fragile silence that hung heavily around her. Her chest tightened with the weight of the heart, still beating steadily beneath her skin, its pulse unyielding, its rhythm slow and deliberate. It was no longer merely a force she could feel—it was her.

The darkness was everywhere. It curled around the edges of her vision like a fog, twisting through the air, creeping into the deepest corners of her mind. It pressed in from all sides, smothering her, and Lily was no longer sure where the shadows ended and she began.

She moved, though her body was numb, every step feeling heavier than the last. She wasn't sure what drove her to keep walking—whether it was the sheer force of the heart's power or the crushing need to escape the suffocating grip of the darkness that clung to her. But she moved. Slowly, deliberately, like a puppet with invisible strings.

A sound—soft, barely perceptible—reached her ears. A whisper that seemed to float through the air, like a breeze, or a memory. She froze, her heart hammering painfully in her chest.

No, not again.

The voice.

Her mind screamed at her to run, to escape, to resist, but it was too late. She could feel the presence before she even saw him. The weight of his gaze pressed into her back, cold and unrelenting, pulling her attention toward him, drawing her deeper into the abyss.

Lily didn't turn around. She couldn't.

"You're still running," the voice said, a dark laugh threading through his words. It was the man—the one who had haunted her thoughts, the one who had bound her to the heart. "But where can you run when the darkness is inside you?"

She felt the words like a physical blow, a sharp sting that echoed through her veins. The power of the heart reacted, thrumming beneath her skin in response, hungry, urgent. She stumbled forward, her hands outstretched, trying to steady herself, trying to regain control. But it was useless. The more she tried to fight it, the more it consumed her.

The heart was alive.

"You know," the man continued, his footsteps echoing behind her, "when I first saw you, I thought you'd be different. I thought you'd resist longer. But you're already giving in."

Lily's throat tightened. Her fingers brushed against the pendant once again, the cool metal pressing into her palm, but it wasn't comfort anymore. It was an anchor, dragging her deeper into the sea of shadows that pulled at her every step.

"I never wanted this," she gasped, the words escaping her throat in a frantic rush. "I never asked for this power."

The man chuckled softly, the sound dark and cruel. "No one ever asks for power. But it's the heart that chooses, not you. And once it chooses, you're already too far gone to turn back. You can't fight it, Lily. You never could."

Her vision swam, her mind clouded with the intensity of his words, with the weight of the heart's power growing within her. She tried to push back, to focus on anything other than him, but her body betrayed her. She could feel the shadows—feel him—drawing closer, an invisible force that pulled at her like a magnet.

Suddenly, her legs buckled. She collapsed to the floor, the impact of her body hitting the ground sending shockwaves of pain through her. The pendant burned against her chest, its heat searing through her, and she cried out in agony, the darkness inside her flaring in response. She gasped for breath, every inhale a struggle, as though the air itself had become thick and suffocating.

"Get up," the man's voice was closer now, soft and commanding. His tone was like silk—smooth, persuasive—but there was an edge to it. "Get up, Lily. You're not done yet. You've only just begun."

Lily's hands trembled as she pushed herself off the ground, every movement a battle against the pain that tore through her body. She could feel the darkness clinging to her, crawling under her skin, in her veins, suffocating her from the inside out.

"You don't understand," she managed to say through gritted teeth. "This isn't me. This isn't who I am."

The man's shadow loomed over her, and for the briefest moment, Lily could see his face. His eyes—dark, cold, and calculating—locked onto hers, and a shiver ran down her spine. He was too close, too real, and the heart seemed to pulse in time with the rhythm of her panic.

"I understand more than you think," he whispered, his voice barely more than a breath, yet it felt like the weight of a thousand worlds pressing down on her. "I've always known who you were. Who you are. And now, it's time for you to know, too."

Lily felt her body seize up, the darkness within her surging with power, demanding to be freed. Her chest tightened as the heart pulsed again, a violent, frantic beat that resonated through her bones. It wasn't her anymore. It wasn't just the heart—it was him, the man who had set this all in motion. He had been there from the very beginning, pulling the strings, manipulating her into becoming something she could barely recognize.

"You've known all along," the man continued, his voice cruel in its certainty. "You've always felt the pull. The heart chose you for a reason. It is you. And now you must fulfill your destiny."

Lily's breath quickened, panic flooding her system. Destiny? She had never asked for this—never wanted it. She had tried so hard to hold onto the pieces of herself, to resist the darkness, but with each passing moment, it was slipping through her fingers, out of her control.

"I won't be your puppet," she gasped, her voice raw with desperation.

The man's expression softened, but there was no kindness in his eyes. "No, you won't be a puppet. You'll be something far greater. Something more powerful than you could ever imagine."

Lily's body trembled with the weight of his words. She could feel it—feel the heart's power pulsing inside her, urging her to give in, to embrace what it had become. She wanted to scream, wanted to fight, but she was so tired. Every part of her was exhausted. And the darkness... it was so close, so overwhelming. She could almost taste it on the tip of her tongue.

"I don't want this," she whispered, the words barely audible.

The man's lips curled into a smile, one that held no warmth.

"It doesn't matter what you want anymore."

The shadows around her grew darker, denser. The air grew thick, oppressive. Her vision blurred as the darkness pressed in, threatening to swallow her whole. She could hear the whispers again, louder now, insistent. The heart was calling to her, pulling her closer to the edge.

It was too late.

As the darkness closed in, Lily felt her soul begin to unravel. There was no escaping it. No way back.

The man's voice echoed through the void.

"Welcome to your true self."

# 25

# Beneath the Surface

Lily's world shifted.

She couldn't tell if it was the ground or herself that had tilted. Everything was spinning—dizzying, suffocating—and the pressure in her chest felt like it might collapse her entire being. The shadows pressed in from all sides, thick and suffocating, wrapping themselves around her like invisible hands, pulling her deeper into something she could no longer escape.

Her heartbeat had quickened, pounding against her ribs, each thud a sharp reminder of what was happening, what was slipping away from her.

You are no longer in control.

The words echoed in her mind, spoken by the man, the one who had always been just beyond her reach. His presence was a constant hum in the back of her mind, like a reminder that no matter how hard she tried to break free, there was no way out. No way back.

She could hear the pulse of the heart now, louder than ever, its rhythm synchronized with her own, like two hearts, two souls beating as one. It was a sickening sound. It was as if the world had faded to black, and there was nothing left but her and the heartbeat, growing ever more insistent.

Breathe. Focus. Think.

Her eyes shot open. The darkness that had once been a vague, abstract threat now felt real, its tendrils curling around her vision like a living thing, demanding her attention. The man—him—was somewhere near, she could feel his presence like a cold gust of wind on the back of her neck. She wasn't sure if he was truly here, or if the connection between them had become so deep, so twisted, that his presence now existed within the very air she breathed.

Every breath she took felt heavy, laden with the weight of the heart's magic. She wasn't just a vessel anymore—she was the magic. It coursed through her veins like liquid fire, swirling beneath her skin, scorching her from the inside out.

She could feel it.

The power. The darkness.

The hunger.

It was undeniable.

A flash of movement caught her eye. She turned quickly, and there—standing just beyond the threshold of the room—was a shadow. But it wasn't just any shadow. This one moved with purpose, as if it were aware of her, aware of her.

She froze.

It wasn't him.

It wasn't the man. This figure, darker than the night itself, exuded a different kind of power. It was wild, untamed, almost animalistic. Its eyes glowed faintly, burning with an intensity that sent a shiver crawling down her spine. It wasn't human.

It was something else.

The shadows around Lily shifted, writhing like snakes, but this time, she didn't feel the crushing weight of them. She felt them receding, like the very darkness itself was afraid. The figure's eyes locked onto hers, and Lily's breath caught in her throat. There was something deep in those eyes—something old. Something that felt familiar.

"Who are you?" she whispered, her voice shaky. Her body was trembling uncontrollably, but her mind was clear. For the first time in what felt like forever, she could see past the veil of shadows, and in front of her was a presence—a force—that wasn't a part of the heart's dark grip.

The figure stepped closer, its movement smooth, as if the very air bent around it. Every step it took sent ripples through the atmosphere, warping the shadows around them like they were nothing more than mist. It was both terrifying and magnetic, drawing her in, making her want to reach out and understand it, even as every instinct screamed at her to run.

"I don't want to hurt you," the figure spoke, its voice low and resonant, like thunder rumbling beneath the earth. "But you are not what you think you are."

Lily's heart stuttered. The words—those simple words—made her feel as though her entire world had shifted once again. The ground beneath her feet seemed to vanish for a moment, replaced by an overwhelming sensation of vertigo.

What did it mean? What was she? What was happening to her?

She opened her mouth to speak, but the words wouldn't come. The figure's eyes narrowed, a flicker of something almost like recognition passing through them, before it spoke again.

"You are not alone in this, Lily. The darkness does not own you."

She could hear the conviction in its voice, and for a moment, Lily dared to hope. Maybe there was a way out. Maybe she could still escape the suffocating grip of the heart. But before she could process the thought, the shadows thickened again, surging forward like a tidal wave, driven by an unseen force.

Her hand instinctively went to the pendant, the cold metal burning against her skin. But this time, the sensation wasn't the usual searing pain. This time, it was different. The pendant pulsed in her palm, the thrum of the heart resonating through her entire being. She could feel the shift—it was shifting.

The shadows had returned, but this time, they were no longer silent. They moved with a new purpose, writhing in sync with the rhythm of the heart. It was as if the entire world had begun to fold in on itself, converging on the moment when Lily would have to make her choice.

The figure—it—watched her, unmoving, its eyes glowing faintly, like twin orbs of fire in the dark. It didn't speak again. It didn't need to. The choice was now hers.

The shadows around her were closing in again, but Lily was no longer afraid. She wasn't sure why—perhaps it was the figure, or maybe the heart, or even the voice of the man that still echoed in the back of her mind. Whatever it was, something had shifted within her. The chaos was still there—the heart still throbbed, its power still pulsating within her, clawing to be freed—but for the first time, she could feel the weight of her own decision.

Could she fight back?

Could she control it?

Her pulse quickened again as she stood on the edge of the abyss, her hands trembling at her sides. The power was overwhelming, but it wasn't just the heart. It was the truth that had been buried deep within her, hidden beneath layers of fear and denial.

The truth that she was stronger than she had ever realized.

She took a step forward.

The shadows recoiled, retreating like a wounded animal, as if they could feel her resolve. Lily stood tall now, her breathing steadying, the overwhelming pressure in her chest beginning to ease. The figure—no longer a stranger, but something much more important—watched her, its expression unreadable.

"You don't have to be afraid," it said softly. "The darkness only has power over you if you let it."

Lily's hand tightened around the pendant. She didn't know if she was ready, if she had the strength to face what was coming, but for the first time, she wasn't consumed by the heart's power.

For the first time, she was in control.

## 26

## The Price of Freedom

Lily could feel it—everything was shifting. Her fingers were still wrapped tightly around the pendant, the cold metal a constant reminder of the heart that beat in unison with hers. The rhythm was a strange comfort, but it was also a heavy burden, its pull stronger than ever. The shadows had receded, but they were waiting, lurking just beyond her vision, as if anticipating her next move.

Her breath came in shallow gasps. She was aware of the figure in front of her, though its presence was less imposing now. It was no longer just a shadow in the corner of her eye. No, now it was something more—a tangible, undeniable force that she couldn't escape, but strangely didn't want to.

Her heart—her true heart—was pounding, and she could feel every inch of it. The magic, the darkness, the power—everything swirled together in a way that made her dizzy. But through the chaos, she understood one thing clearly: she was standing at a precipice, her every decision now leading her closer to a fate she couldn't predict.

The figure spoke again, its voice soft but carrying weight. "You've only just begun to understand what's at stake, Lily. But you can still change the course of everything. There's a way out. A way to free yourself from all of this."

She opened her mouth to respond, but her voice caught in her throat. What could she say? The words felt meaningless now, even though they had been her refuge for so long. What if it was too late to go back? What if there was no escape from the darkness that had consumed her?

"You can break free," the figure pressed, its glowing eyes never leaving hers. "You don't have to be its vessel. You don't have to be the one who carries this burden."

The offer hung between them, tantalizing and impossible. Could she really escape the power? Could she walk away from the heart without it consuming her whole? She could feel it inside of her, pulsing and thrumming, a living thing. It was part of her now, as much as her breath, her pulse. The longer she held onto it, the more it was becoming her.

But freedom...

Lily glanced down at the pendant again, watching the way it shimmered in the dim light, its surface reflecting the flickering flames that danced in the room. For a moment, she couldn't breathe, couldn't think. She wanted to reach out and destroy it, to end the madness. But there was something inside of her—a voice—telling her that without the heart, she would lose everything.

Without the heart, there was nothing.

"Do you hear it?" the figure asked, its tone softer now, as if coaxing her to listen. "The heart doesn't care about you. It doesn't care about your soul, your desires. It cares only about its own survival. It will take everything from you, Lily. And when you have nothing left, it will leave you empty, hollow. You'll be a shell of who you once were. It will control you."

Her fingers dug into the pendant, her nails biting into the cold metal. She could feel the weight of its power, but with that weight came the truth. The truth she had been refusing to face for so long.

She wasn't its master. She was its slave.

The shadows stirred again, as if reacting to her inner turmoil. They shifted, faster now, like a swirling vortex, closing in on her from every angle. They didn't just want her—they needed her. And Lily knew it. She had been chosen for a reason, bound to the heart in a way that was deeper than fate, than chance. The heart and its darkness were woven into her very existence now.

The figure stepped forward, and Lily flinched. There was something almost sorrowful in its gaze, something that spoke of pain she could not yet understand. "You don't have to carry this alone," it said, each word a soft caress in the midst of the storm. "There is a cost, but it's one you can bear. You don't have to give it everything. You don't have to lose yourself."

"Tell me how," Lily's voice cracked as she finally found her words. The desperation in her tone made her chest tighten. She was at the edge of the abyss. She didn't know if she could pull herself back, or if she even wanted to.

The figure hesitated, its eyes flickering, before it stepped even closer, so close that Lily could feel the heat of its presence, the almost tangible weight of the moment. "The cost, Lily," it whispered, "is your heart."

Lily's eyes widened, her pulse hammering in her throat. "What do you mean?" she gasped, the words slipping from her lips before she could stop them. "I can't... I can't give it up. I can't."

The figure sighed deeply, its form almost flickering like a wisp of smoke in the dim light. "You can't hold onto the heart and retain yourself. You can't both keep your humanity and carry its weight. To free yourself from its grasp, you must make a choice."

The words settled in the air between them like poison, and Lily felt a chill run down her spine. There was a cost—a terrible price—and it was one she couldn't avoid. The heart was a force of nature, and to remove it would mean ripping apart the very fabric of her soul. But to keep it would mean surrendering to something darker, something deeper, something that would eventually swallow her whole.

It wasn't just the heart. It was her.

"I can't," she whispered, her hands trembling as they moved to her chest, her fingers brushing against the pendant. "I can't let go of it."

The figure's eyes softened. "Then you will lose yourself, Lily. You'll become a puppet, a vessel for something that doesn't care about you. A tool of destruction. You'll be nothing more than a whisper in the wind."

Her breath caught in her throat as the shadows around her began to swirl faster, drawing tighter, closing in like the jaws of some unseen beast. The air felt thick with pressure, suffocating her, and she could hear the heartbeat in her chest now, so loud that it was the only sound in the world.

It was coming for her.

The figure stood motionless, watching her, waiting for her choice.

There was no escape, no turning back. The darkness was all around her, inside her. And the price of freedom? It was her very soul. The heart that had become part of her, that had woven itself into every fiber of her being, was both her curse and her salvation.

She had no choice.

Lily closed her eyes, squeezing them tight against the tears she could feel welling up. The shadows whispered, the heart throbbed, and the cost—the price—was too high to bear. But there was no choice anymore.

With trembling hands, she lifted the pendant from her chest, its weight nearly too much to bear, and as her fingers wrapped around it, she felt the darkness surge once more. The moment had come.

And she let it go.

The world shattered.

# 27

# Fractured Souls

The silence that followed was deafening.

Lily's heart, once so steady and steadying, had stopped. The absence of its familiar pulse left her breathless. A terrible void opened inside her, vast and consuming. It felt like the very foundation of her existence had cracked and splintered, leaving her suspended in a place that was neither here nor there. She couldn't breathe. She couldn't think. All that remained was the hollow echo of the decision she'd just made, reverberating through the air, thick with the weight of its finality.

The pendant—now cold and inert in her hand—was nothing more than metal, a lifeless thing. It was no longer the source of power. It no longer pulsed with the heartbeat of the dark force that had once controlled her. The power that had been tied to her very soul, that had danced in her blood and sung in her veins, was gone.

And with it, so too was the man.

She could feel the absence of him. The connection had snapped, severed like a rope that had been cut clean through, leaving only the jagged edges of what had once been a bond she couldn't break, no matter how hard she tried. It was as though the very air around her had lost its substance, as if the world was slowly folding into itself.

Lily swayed on her feet, her body trembling with the sudden emptiness. She wanted to scream, to feel something, anything. But nothing came. Her voice, once so full of passion and fear and anger, had vanished with the heart's power. She was a ghost now, a shadow of her former self.

The darkness—the shadows—stirred around her, swirling, but this time, it was different. They were no longer a reflection of the heart, but of something else entirely. They were alive, sentient, and they recoiled from her, as if afraid, as if sensing that she was no longer their master. But their fear didn't mean they were gone. They were still here, still watching, still waiting.

Lily stumbled backward, her legs weak beneath her. She reached for the nearest support, her hands grasping at the edge of a cold stone wall. She needed to steady herself, needed to focus, but her mind was racing, thrumming with a thousand thoughts that collided into one another, too fast to process. What had she done? What had she really done?

The price of freedom.

The words, spoken so softly by the figure, echoed in her mind, taunting her with their meaning. She had let go of the heart, the dark power that had bound her to the world, and in doing so, had stripped herself of everything that made her whole. The price wasn't just the heart—it was herself. It was her very essence, her soul.

She looked down at her hands, as though expecting to see something—anything—that was different. But there was nothing. No sign of the magic that had once thrummed beneath her skin. No trace of the power that had once controlled her. It was gone.

And then, the shadows thickened.

It happened so quickly. One moment, the room was still, and then—

A flicker. A movement. Something in the air, a shift too subtle to name, but unmistakable.

A figure stepped out of the dark corner of the room. It was the same figure, the one that had warned her, the one that had told her of the cost. But now it was different. It was no longer just a shadow, no longer a mere whisper in the dark. It was real, tangible, its presence unmistakable. Its eyes burned with a soft, unsettling glow, and its form seemed to pulse, almost as if it were alive, changing, shifting with every step it took.

"You've done it," the figure said, its voice a deep, echoing murmur, as if spoken from far away and yet right beside her. "You've let go of the heart. But you don't understand what that means."

Lily's breath hitched. She wanted to speak, but her throat was dry, her tongue thick. What could she say? What could she ask? Her body still trembled with the aftershocks of the decision she had made, but now, with the figure in front of her, a new fear gripped her heart. Was it too late? Had she made a mistake?

"No," the figure said, reading her mind with an ease that made Lily's skin crawl. "It is not too late to fix this. But know this, Lily—the heart was not just a power you could wield. It was a part of you, a part that you cannot simply erase. It has left its mark, and that mark will never fade."

Lily's fingers tightened around the pendant, still in her hand, now cold and silent. The mark. What did it mean? What had she done?

"The shadows, the darkness—it was all a part of you," the figure continued, its voice growing darker, more insistent. "You thought you could escape it, that by letting go of the heart, you could free yourself. But there is no freedom from this."

Lily shook her head, as if to clear it, as if to push away the suffocating truth. "What do you mean?" Her voice was barely a whisper, but the words were edged with desperation.

The figure moved closer, its presence overwhelming, suffocating. "I mean that you have fractured your soul, Lily. You cannot exist without the heart. You cannot simply sever the bond and remain whole. The very thing you have cast aside has become part of your being. And now, it will take what is owed."

Her heart thudded painfully in her chest, each beat louder than the last. "What... what will happen to me?"

The figure's gaze softened for a moment, but the shadow of something darker flickered in its eyes. "You will feel the emptiness. The hunger. It will consume you. But that is not the worst of it." It paused, and Lily felt her stomach twist, the air growing thick around them. "The heart is no longer just a part of you. It is seeking."

Lily's eyes widened, panic surging through her veins. "Seeking? Seeking what?"

The figure did not answer immediately. Instead, it moved closer, as if compelled by an unseen force. "The heart is not gone. It will never be gone. You cannot escape it, not now, not ever."

The darkness around her surged forward, and Lily's body tensed. The shadows wrapped around her like a noose, pulling tighter with every breath she took. Her legs buckled beneath her, and she collapsed to the floor, gasping for air.

The figure's voice was low and foreboding as it spoke again. "The heart will always find its way back to you, Lily. And when it does, it will not be the same."

Lily's eyes darted around the room, the shadows closing in, suffocating her, as if they could feel the truth in her soul, a truth she was just beginning to understand. The heart—the power, the darkness—was not something she could escape. Not anymore.

And in that moment, Lily understood the final, terrible truth:

She had never been free. Not really. She had only delayed the inevitable.

The heart would come for her.

And when it did, it would take everything.

# 28

# The Hunt Begins

The world was slipping away, piece by piece, like sand through her fingers.

Lily's mind reeled as the shadows stretched and twisted around her, cold tendrils reaching into the very marrow of her bones. She could feel the familiar pull, that tug of something ancient and relentless, calling to her from the depths of her soul. The heart—the heart she had cast aside—was still there, still tethered to her like an invisible chain. It had never truly left. It was always going to find her.

The figure stood over her, its eyes glowing with an eerie, predatory light, watching as Lily tried to breathe through the suffocating pressure that surrounded her. She could feel the weight of it—the darkness, the malevolent energy—it pressed against her chest, making each breath feel like a battle.

"You think you can run?" The figure's voice was low and mocking, its words cutting through the suffocating air. "You think you can escape the thing that is tied to your very essence? The heart will always find you, no matter where you go. No matter what you do."

Lily's heart pounded in her chest, a frantic rhythm of fear and panic. She struggled to push herself to her feet, her hands trembling as they pressed against the cold stone of the floor. The darkness was closing in, tightening around her, and every instinct in her body screamed that it was too late. Too late to escape.

"You've already made your choice, Lily," the figure continued, its tone heavy with a dark satisfaction. "Now, there's no going back. The heart will come for you. It will hunt you, and when it does, it will take everything you have. Everything."

Lily's mind raced, her thoughts a blur of confusion and dread. She had thought she could break free, that she could destroy the heart and walk away from all of this. But she had been wrong. The heart was never going to let her go. It had always been part of her. And now, it was coming back for what it had lost.

A cold chill ran through her as the figure stepped forward, its presence more oppressive than ever. Its form was shifting, wavering, like smoke in the wind, and Lily could feel the pressure growing—like the very air around her was being sucked into a void.

"You've opened the door, Lily," the figure hissed. "Now, you will face the consequences. The heart will return to you, and when it does, you will no longer be the same. It will take more than your soul. It will take everything—your humanity, your very being."

Lily's mind screamed in protest, her body trembling with a combination of fear and anger. No, this couldn't be happening. She wouldn't let it. She couldn't. She had already made the choice to rid herself of the heart, to escape its pull, but now... now it was too late.

The shadows shifted again, and Lily was suddenly surrounded by an oppressive darkness. It was no longer just a presence in the room. It was alive, moving, swirling around her, pulling at her, dragging her into its depths. She could hear the sound of something distant, something familiar, pulsing from within the darkness—a heartbeat, rhythmic and steady, like a drum in the distance.

It was the heart.

The shadows were closing in, suffocating her, and Lily could feel herself being dragged forward, her feet slipping, her body weightless as if she were caught in an endless descent. Her head spun, her breath quickening, as she tried to steady herself, but the pressure was too much. The walls of the room seemed to bend and stretch, warping into dark, shifting shapes.

Then, suddenly, there was a pull—a sharp tug at her chest, deep within her very being. She gasped, her hands instinctively clutching at her heart as if to stop it from escaping, but the feeling was not hers to control. It wasn't her hand holding the reins anymore. It was the heart, the darkness, pulling her toward it.

The ground beneath her feet disappeared entirely.

Lily fell, her body weightless as if in a dream. The room, the figure, everything faded into nothingness as she was consumed by the darkness. Her mind raced, trying to understand what was happening, but all she could feel was the pressure on her chest. The thrum of the heart, louder now, as if it were calling to her. It was no longer just a part of her—it was controlling her, pulling her into the black abyss.

And then, she was standing.

The shadows surrounded her, the air thick with their presence, but the weight on her chest had shifted. It was different now. The heart, the very thing she had thought she had destroyed, was back—alive and pulsing with an energy that was alien and ancient. It was inside her again, but it was more than that. It was against her. She could feel it, clawing at her insides, digging deeper with every passing second.

A voice echoed in the darkness, distant but unmistakable.

"You cannot escape me, Lily."

Her head snapped around, her heart racing in her chest. There was no one in the room with her. No figure. No presence. But the voice—that voice—was everywhere, inside her, around her. It was the heart speaking. It was aware. It was conscious.

The world around her shifted again, and she felt herself moving—being dragged by the very force that had once been her own. It was no longer just the power she had controlled; it was the force that now controlled her.

"You cannot run," the voice continued, its tone cold, merciless. "You were always meant to carry this burden, Lily. You cannot cast me aside. I am part of you."

Lily stumbled, her hands clutching at her chest, gasping for air, but there was no air to be had. The pressure was unbearable, like a weight pressing on her chest, squeezing her heart, forcing it to beat in time with the thrum of the darkness.

"You think you are free," the voice whispered again, closer now, right next to her ear. "But there is no freedom. There never was."

The darkness around her pulsed, alive with the heartbeat that resonated through her body, louder, faster, filling her mind with its rhythm, its power. She could feel the hunger, the insatiable pull of the heart, dragging her toward the one thing she had fought so desperately to avoid.

It was coming.

It was coming for her.

And there was nowhere to hide.

Lily's heart raced, but now it was not her own. It was the heart's pulse, quickening, faster, the rhythm impossible to outrun. She was caught in its grip, its power too strong, too absolute. It was closing in on her, surrounding her, consuming her.

And in that moment, Lily knew the truth:

She had never been free.

The heart had always been a part of her, and now it was hunting her.

The hunt had begun.

# 29

# A Heart's Betrayal

The air was suffocating, thick with the weight of the darkness that seemed to pulse around Lily, pressing down on her like the sky itself had collapsed. She staggered forward, her legs weak, every step heavy as though the very ground beneath her was pulling her down into the earth. The heartbeat, that maddening, rhythmic pulse that had once been her power, now echoed within her like the sound of an ancient drum. It was relentless, unyielding, and it was coming from the depths of her soul.

It's inside me. It's controlling me.

Lily's thoughts spiraled, disoriented and frantic. She had felt it the moment the darkness had taken her—she had felt the heart slither back inside her, wrapping itself around her insides like a serpent, its tendrils sinking deeper into her flesh. It was there, in the very core of her, and it had no intention of letting go.

Her breath came in shallow gasps, her hands trembling as she reached for the walls around her, her fingers brushing against the cold stone that felt alive beneath her touch. The room was shifting, warping, as if it too were a reflection of her mind—a mirror of the madness she was trapped in. The shadows moved, swirling around her like hungry predators, waiting for the moment she let her guard down, ready to tear her apart.

Lily closed her eyes, trying to steady her breath, trying to think clearly, but the pressure inside her chest only grew heavier with every passing second. She was being consumed, and there was nothing she could do to stop it. The heart had taken everything—her body, her soul—and now it was taking control of her very will.

And yet, there was something else. Something that made her blood run cold.

A whisper, faint but unmistakable, slithered through the darkness. It was a voice. A voice she had not heard in so long, one that should have been gone—his voice.

"Lily..."

She froze.

Her heart skipped a beat. She wanted to look around, to see if anyone was there, but the shadows closed in, wrapping around her, twisting her vision. The voice was a distant murmur, but it was enough to send a chill crawling down her spine.

"Lily... you've made a mistake."

It wasn't the figure's voice. It was different. It was deeper, more familiar. And though it was barely a whisper, it carried the weight of a thousand secrets. The voice of the one she thought was gone. The one who had betrayed her.

Her chest tightened, a sharp pain racing through her. No, this couldn't be happening. Not now. Not when everything had already spiraled out of control. She tried to shake off the fear, to find the strength to move, to fight back. But the heart's presence inside her was suffocating, overwhelming. The shadows laughed in her mind, and the voice continued to taunt her.

"You never thought you could outrun me, did you?"

Her breath caught in her throat, and for a moment, she could barely breathe. The voice seemed to echo from within her, pulling at her very thoughts, tugging her toward something she couldn't understand. Something she didn't want to understand.

"You made the wrong choice, Lily," the voice purred, closer now, as though it were right behind her, whispering against her ear. "You think you can escape the heart? You think you can cast it aside, make it your enemy? But you are its servant. You always have been. It knows you. It owns you."

Lily's pulse quickened, her hands gripping the stone so hard that her knuckles turned white. The shadows pressed in, the heartbeat within her chest quickening, matching the rhythm of the voice that was crawling under her skin, wrapping itself around her thoughts.

"No..." she gasped, shaking her head in denial. "I am free. I—I let go of it. I—"

Her voice faltered. The room shifted again, and for a split second, she saw him. Just for a heartbeat, she saw the man she had loved—the man who had once been everything to her—his face twisted in shadow, a cruel smirk curling on his lips.

"You thought you could live without me?" His voice dripped with contempt, and the shadows around her grew thicker, darker, as though they were feeding off the malice that radiated from him. "Foolish girl. You can't survive without your heart. You were never meant to be free. Not from me."

Lily's breath caught in her throat. The pain, the anger—it felt so real, like the weight of betrayal had never truly lifted from her. But she couldn't let him control her—not again. She couldn't let the darkness swallow her whole.

"Stop," she gasped, her voice breaking, the words fighting their way through the tightness in her chest. "I'm not yours. I won't let you do this."

The shadows surged forward, tightening their grip on her, dragging her deeper into the darkness. She fought, she struggled, her hands scrambling against the walls, but there was no escape. The heartbeat within her had become deafening, an unbearable roar in her ears, and the voice of the man who had once held her heart was drowning her.

"You're already mine, Lily," he whispered, his voice like a

lover's caress, but laced with venom. "You always were."

The pressure in her chest intensified, a vice that squeezed tighter with every breath she tried to take. The shadows wrapped around her legs, pulling her down, forcing her to her knees. She looked down at her hands, trembling, as they clenched in desperation. Her skin felt foreign, as though the very fibers of her being were unraveling. The heart inside her—the heart—it was no longer just a tool or a power. It was something darker, something that knew her, that had always known her.

She could feel it now, could feel the pulse of it, the weight of it, dragging her back toward the abyss. But this time, something was different. This time, the heart was her. It was everything she had been, everything she was. There was no distinction anymore.

"You cannot escape your fate," the voice murmured again, a dark promise that shivered along her spine. "The heart is inside you, and it will never let you go. Not now. Not ever."

A chill ran through Lily, and for a fleeting moment, she considered giving in. The weight of the darkness around her was so heavy, so overwhelming. It would be so easy to surrender to it. To let the heart take control again. To let it wash over her, take the pain away, pull her into the blackness.

But something deep inside her—a spark, a faint glimmer—flickered to life. No. She couldn't let it happen. She couldn't let herself be consumed again. She had to fight, had to find a way to reclaim herself.

The shadows pulled tighter, the heartbeat louder, but Lily held on to the only thing she had left.

Her will.

With everything she had, she pushed against the darkness, against the pull of the heart, against the voice that whispered in her ear. Her fingers dug into the stone, her nails scraping against the surface as she fought to stay grounded.

The world trembled around her. The shadows surged. But Lily would not let go. She wouldn't surrender.

Not again.

Not to him. Not to the heart.

She was more than this.

She had to be.

But the darkness had already begun to laugh.

ID # The Final Choice

*Lily's breath came in ragged gasps as she stumbled through the twisted labyrinth of darkness that surrounded her. The shadows seemed to pulse and writhe with a life of their own, whispering in tongues she couldn't understand, their murmurs thick with malice. Her heart, that damned, cursed organ, thudded painfully against her chest, matching the rhythm of the pulse that filled the very air around her. The darkness felt alive, suffocating her with its hunger, its need to swallow her whole.*

The heartbeat had become unbearable, an echo that reverberated through every inch of her body, as though her very soul was being tugged toward something far darker than she had ever imagined. The air smelled of ash and decay, thick with an ancient, unspoken promise—the promise of ruin, of destruction.

*It's coming. It's going to consume me.*

Her body trembled, a mix of fear and defiance warring within her. She had fought so hard, so desperately, to escape this fate, to rid herself of the heart's cruel grasp. But it had always been a lie. The heart was never something she could simply cast aside. It was part of her. And now, it was pulling her toward the very end, its power growing stronger with each passing moment.

Lily clenched her fists, digging her nails into her palms as if the pain could center her, could pull her back from the brink of madness. She had to stop it. She had to find a way to break free. But the shadows were closing in, twisting tighter around her, pulling her deeper into their dark embrace. The room—the world—was shifting, warping, bending in on itself. She was no longer sure what was real.

And then, she saw him.

The figure emerged from the swirling darkness like a ghost, his silhouette barely visible against the inky void. He was the last thing she had wanted to see. The man who had betrayed her, who had taken everything from her, now stood before her, his presence filling the room like a suffocating weight.

His eyes, once warm and full of love, were now cold, distant, and unreadable. His mouth curled into a smile—taunting, cruel.

"You still think you can escape this, don't you?" His voice echoed through her mind, sending a shiver of dread down her spine. "You can't outrun fate, Lily. You never could."

Lily's heart skipped a beat. She wanted to run, wanted to fight, but her body wouldn't move. She was rooted to the spot, her legs unwilling to obey her commands. The shadows seemed to hold her in place, the weight of his presence dragging her down into an abyss from which there was no return.

"No," she gasped, the word barely escaping her lips. "You're not real. You're just a part of the darkness. You can't control me."

The figure laughed, a low, hollow sound that echoed through the air, causing the very walls around her to tremble. "Control you? I don't need to control you, Lily. I never did. The heart is what controls you now. It always has. You were always meant to be its vessel, to carry its power. You never had a choice."

His words sliced through her like a blade, and she could feel the coldness of them seep into her bones. It was true. The heart had been with her from the very beginning, a constant presence, a dark echo in the back of her mind. It had shaped her, molded her, and now it was coming for her, hungry and relentless.

"No!" she screamed, shaking her head. "I am not its servant. I am not yours!"

The figure stepped closer, his gaze never leaving hers. His

eyes seemed to burn with a cold fire, an unspoken threat in their depths.

"You think you're free?" he asked, his voice barely a whisper. "You're nothing without it, Lily. The heart is you. And you will always be mine. Always."

The words hit her like a physical blow, sending her stumbling backward. She could feel the darkness rising up to meet her, the very air around her pressing in, suffocating her. Her vision blurred, and the heartbeat—so loud, so insistent—was drowning her in its rhythm. It was the sound of her own destruction, the sound of everything she had fought to escape.

But then, something inside her shifted.

A flicker.

A spark.

The darkness pressed in closer, the shadows drawing tighter around her, but this time, Lily didn't fight. She didn't resist. Instead, she closed her eyes and focused. Deep within her, she could feel the heart—its cold, brutal power, its unrelenting force. She could feel it thrumming, pulsing with a life of its own. It was part of her, yes. But it was also more than that. It was a part of something older, something deeper.

And in that moment, she understood.

The heart wasn't just something she could destroy. It was a power—a force that connected her to everything around her. It wasn't about controlling it. It was about *embracing* it.

She took a deep breath, feeling the weight of the darkness around her, and for the first time, she welcomed it. The shadows that had once threatened to consume her now wrapped around her like a cloak, like a familiar, cold embrace. She could feel the pulse of the heart inside her, beating in time with her own breath.

And then she looked at the figure—the man who had once been everything to her.

"No," she said, her voice steady now, stronger than she had ever felt. "You never had control over me. Not then. Not now."

The figure recoiled, his face contorted with disbelief, as though her words had struck him in a way he had never expected. He took a step back, his eyes narrowing, but there was no longer any confidence in his stance. There was only fear.

"You don't understand," he hissed, the words like poison. "You can't wield this power. It will destroy you."

Lily's eyes never left him as she took a slow step forward. The shadows parted around her like water parting before a storm. She could feel the heart beating, not just within her, but around her—its power flooding through the very air. She was no longer afraid. She was no longer trapped.

"Maybe I don't understand," she said, her voice quiet but unwavering. "But I don't need to. I have the choice now. And I choose to control it."

In that moment, the shadows flared, a storm of darkness crashing around them. The figure's eyes widened in shock as the darkness surged forward, swallowing him whole. His scream echoed through the air, but it was cut short, replaced by a silence so complete, it was as though he had never been there at all.

Lily stood alone in the stillness, her chest heaving as she breathed in the air around her. The heart was still there, still beating within her, but it no longer controlled her. She had taken control of it. She had made her choice.

And for the first time in a long time, Lily was free.